DATA
VALUE
SUCCESS

DRAMATICALLY DIFFERENT DATA
DISCOURSE DONE DRYLY & DYNAMICALLY

v1.0

PAUL DANIEL JONES

Copyright © 2022 Paul Daniel Jones

http://www.pauldanieljones.com

All rights reserved. No part of this book may be reproduced or used in any manner without written permission of the copyright owner except for the use of quotations in a book review.

ISBN: 9798352176450

DEDICATION

To my colleagues at Baringa Partners.

It's a privilege to work with a group of such talented and experienced people.

Here's to Putting People First, and Delivering Impact that Lasts!

CONTENTS

	Introduction	1
1	Data Management Is Everywhere	7
2	Data Strategy	18
3	Data Leadership	46
4	Data Accountabilities	65
5	Stakeholder Engagement	94
6	Data Governance	106
7	Data Quality	123
8	Data Architecture	141
9	Data Insights & Reporting	160
10	Data Literacy & Data Culture	171
11	Working In Data Management	183
	Conclusion	194
	Acknowledgements	197
	About The Author	198

Introduction

Introduction

Welcome to my book of Data Value Success.

Every page of this book was written for impact, to create:
- a moment of insight,
- a reminder,
- a prompt to take action,
- or even a challenge to be argued with.

And that's because this book is **made entirely of short articles and posts, which I originally posted on LinkedIn**!

Which makes them perfect to dip into, to provoke a new perspective or get some inspiration.

At the time I started compiling this book, I had been publishing content on LinkedIn for more than 5 years (and posting regularly for over a year), but most of that time hadn't been with creating a book in mind, so I was startled to find that the posts hung together really quite well in a sequence (or at least, in a set of logical chapters), without the need for much tweaking.

The great thing about basing this book on LinkedIn posts, is that every single one of them has already been tested with a global audience, and I've only included the posts that resonated with people and provoked positive reactions.

What is this book about?

In short, it is about successfully delivering VALUE through Data Management (hence the title!)

It mainly focuses on the things that really make a difference at a strategic level:
- the **strategy**,
- the **leadership**,
- the **psychology**,
- the people **engagement**,
- and so on…

…but it also includes a sprinkling of subject matter detail, which is also important in any Data Management, Analytics or AI initiative.

There are a few pages that provide **explanations** and **definitions**; a few **stories** and **analogies**; a few posts that are **fun** (even funny) and **thought-provoking**; and all in all, there are lots of **ideas**, which if understood and implemented, will radically improve the chances of any Data initiative's **success**.

Who should read this book?

The main two audiences of this book are:

1. Data Professionals, who are working on the delivery of Data initiatives or advising organisations on them;

2. Senior Executives with an interest in delivering value through Data, or with responsibility for sponsoring a Data initiative.

What will you not get out of this book?

This book is a collection of bite-sized tips about strategic data leadership, so it does NOT provide:
- Comprehensive coverage of all aspects of Data Management;
- Anything really technical: if you're looking for tips on

SQL queries or how to implement different types of statistical regression using R, this isn't the book for you!

What's the best way to read this book?

I have compiled this book to make the articles that I had previously published, easier to access and read. As such, you can read this book in chronological order, and you will gain a rounded view of the insights on each topic.

However, you can also dip into chapters that are of interest to you, or where you are looking for ideas and inspiration on specific topics, to gain value from each page in isolation – because they were all written to work as standalone pieces, before they were brought together here.

Whichever way you choose to read the book, I hope you find its contents interesting, entertaining and valuable.

Here's to your success!

This book is all about making you more successful, by enabling you to deliver more value through data.

So I wish you all the very best on your Data Management journey, and hope the tips in the following pages play some small part in your future achievements.

Before we start, I want to share a bit about why I am so passionate about Data Management…

A Passion for Data Management

Someone asked me the other day: where does my passion for Data Management come from?

How have I managed to keep my enthusiasm, despite all of the challenges in the way of success?

Having held a number of senior corporate data management positions over several years, it struck me that one of the reasons for my successes has been persistence over medium and long time periods.

This tenacity, through changes of sponsorship and business priorities, through various short term emergencies and distractions, has depended on an enduring commitment to a vision for a better future.

So where has this enthusiasm come from?

Put simply: I've actually seen, in the real world, how amazing the impact of effective Data management and analytics can be.

I've seen it at small scale, I've seen in at large scale, and I've seen the massive potential of those successes, should they be replicated and extrapolated to their ultimate end state.

I don't think I would say that I have ever seen the *perfect* solution, in its entirety, but I have seen very good solutions, and I have seen every aspect of the potential whole. I have personally led data initiatives and seen what works and what doesn't; and it's hard to express how incredibly exciting the potential is.

I often meet kindred spirits in different companies, who

have worked in other organisations that are "ahead" of the place they are working now, and we smile knowingly and exchange anecdotes and examples of how simple improvements could drive massive value... as soon as the right sponsorship and priority is put in place to implement those changes.

And it's from this place of not only knowing what's possible, but having been through the hard yards to drive the changes, that my passion comes from. It's never as easy as it should be, but it's always worth it, when it's done properly.

Fellow data management professionals: who's with me on this one?

Part 1: Data Management Is Everywhere

What's Worse Than Bad Data Management?

What's worse: BAD data management, or NO data management?

I'll let you in on a secret:

There's *no such thing* as "NO" data management!

Everything a business does, runs on Data.

So, if you think you've got "NO" data management, either:

- You're managing your Data SO WELL that it's an invisible part of how you operate,

OR (unfortunately, more likely):

- You've not just got BAD data management, you've actually got REALLY BAD data management, which is even worse!

Either way, realising that "managing data" is something all businesses do everywhere, is a useful mindset shift, because if you know that's the case, then you can do something to make it better.

What do you think?

How To Spot Data Management Problems

Are you missing these 5 common but often overlooked signs that indicate that you've got a Data Management problem?

1. Your business is losing money, and you can't work out why

2. You keep getting complaints, and you can't work out why

3. You've got loads of operational problems, and you can't work out why

4. You keep experiencing technology and security incidents, and you can't work out why

5. You're using reports to make business decisions, but you keep getting it wrong

If you "can't work out why", it's probably because you either don't have the Data you need, or you don't have the ability to use it to drive insights and make decisions.

If you are using Data but are still making poor decisions, either the Data is wrong, or you're using it in the wrong way.

Businesses WIN, when they use Data to run their business; to understand how their business is operating; to diagnose problems; and make well-informed business decisions.

Businesses LOSE when they are clutching at straws; operating in the dark; troubleshooting based on gut feel and hearsay.

Are you experiencing any of these problems?

Have you thought about how improving the management and use of Data could help?

Does One-Size-Fits-All Data Management work?

"All Data Management initiatives are essentially the same."

"Every Data Management initiative is different."

BOTH of these statements are TRUE, at the same time.

Can you think of any examples where either of them are false?

THE SAME: Every data management initiative I have ever seen, was setup to address one or more business issues or opportunities, which could be categorised as being one of a set of "common" challenges that many businesses face, and they have also all involved implementing one or more of the standard data management capabilities needed to solve those issues.

DIFFERENT: However, the specific ways in which the issues manifested themselves, for each company, and the specific business impacts, along with the specific ways in which data management capabilities needed to be implemented, to directly and effectively address the issues, were always different.

Any attempt to just generically implement a set of "standard" data management capabilities, without taking into consideration the specifics of the organization, WILL ALMOST CERTAINLY FAIL.

Unfortunately, I have seen this attempted too many times to count, including several examples where very experienced and capable data professionals have fallen into this trap. Often with data professionals, it's either because they've seen something work somewhere before and assume it will work everywhere if it's implemented in exactly the same way, or because they get too wrapped up in the theory and lose their connection to the things that will deliver any real tangible business impacts.

All of the data management capabilities that a data professional will talk about are most likely absolutely the right things to be doing (metadata management, data quality management, reference data management, etc...) However, if they are just implemented in a paint-by-numbers way, they are generally a waste of time.

It's always important to invest the time into understanding the business and its priorities, then develop a strategy for execution that directly addresses those priorities.

Have you seen any examples where paint-by-numbers data management has actually worked? (Or has failed really badly?)

A Bit Of Data Management Optimism

Are you better at Data Management than you think?

I mean, you are still in business, right? You got this far... so you must be doing something right. Every business operates on its data: for example, the ability to contact customers and process payments, depends on having data about those customers and the accounts and values about the payment transactions. This is foundational to any business, so it's got to be happening somehow.

So it's almost impossible not to have some kind of data management practices already in place, even if no-one thinks of it that way.

Which means you've got something to build on.

And if your data management practices are informal and manual and performing badly, then it means that not only do you have something to build on, but delivering improvements to those practices could deliver significant value.

No matter how bad your data management practices are, you're not starting from scratch. Having this mindset can help when starting to tackle problems that may initially seem overwhelmingly large, or engaging with people who need to change and have no idea that they are already managing data in some way.

Every company has data management issues - even the best companies in the world - so don't be discouraged, look for those seeds of good practice and work out how to build on them...

Don't Overlook The Obvious

Sometimes, the most obviously optimal solution is so incredibly obvious, you need someone who's not too close to the problem to spot it.

Sometimes, there's a non-data-management solution that is far better than any data management solution anyone could come up with... and it takes someone who's open to that idea to see it.

Sometimes, a new, cutting-edge, modern solution is the best option.

Sometimes, an older, tried-and-tested approach is better.

What are you doing to make sure you identify and implement the OPTIMAL solution to your business problem?

How are you exploring alternative options and leveraging the right kinds of experiences and skills to get to the best outcomes?

DATA VALUE SUCCESS v1.0

Schedule The Delivery Of Value!

Following the steps in this post could totally transform the effectiveness of your data management investments.

You need to start by asking yourself: WHEN will you realise value from your data initiative?

More specifically: Have you SCHEDULED exactly WHEN you will realise that value?

Or is your plan to "build the foundations" first, and then realise value? Is the "realise value" bit months away?

Is there an option to deliver the value earlier?

Constantly asking yourselves these kinds of questions is the best way to keep focus on the real, tangible outcomes that you're aiming for.

You can pick any data management discipline: data governance, metadata, data lineage, data quality, data literacy... any one of them... it's so easy to invest loads of time and energy "doing them" - but for what?

Whatever data management investment you are making *right now* - think about it for a moment. Can you deliver value through your efforts IN THE NEXT WEEK?

No? How about IN THE NEXT MONTH, then?

In most cases, there is usually some way of delivering something of value in a month, if you really put your mind to it.

How would your plans change, if you really tried to do this?

I'm willing to bet that it could change things quite significantly.

It won't change the need to build sustainable foundations, but it could radically change the *way* you build those foundations; and it could certainly change the speed with which you realise a Return On Investment, and could massively increase the level of trust and support you could build with your business stakeholders.

Give it a go. Look at what you're doing at the moment, ask these questions, and see if you can adjust your plans to deliver some value in a shorter timeframe.

I'm pretty sure you won't regret it.

Information Technology Wouldn't Exist Without Data!

Data has always been an important part of I.T.

It's the "Information" in "Information Technology".

Without it, Information Technology is pointless.

Imagine any piece of I.T. without Data. It simply doesn't do anything.

Which is why I find Technology transformation projects, which focus entirely on the Technology, and don't bother with the Data that the Technology is going to process, totally baffling.

When I studied Computer Science at University, a significant proportion of the courses were focused on Data Structures, Data Warehousing and Knowledge Representation (for Artificial Intelligence and other types of Data processing).

This was long before the "Data" industry existed, as a separate and distinct thing.

Data was just seen as an integral part of computing, because without it, you don't have anything to compute!

I.T. exists to process Data. Business processes are delivered by processing Data. Pretty much anything any of us does, involves Data in some way.

Data Management is something we all do, whether we know it or not.

The question is: do we do it well or not?

Part 2:
Data Strategy

The Strategic Need For Data Management

The great thing about Data Management, is every member of every Executive Committee in every company everywhere could benefit from it (if delivered in the right way).

Just to take two common examples of C-suite / ExCo members and the business outcomes they could benefit from:

Chief Financial Officer (CFO) - more efficient, more reliable financial control and reporting, with less need for manual reconciliation and adjustments

Chief Marketing Officer (CMO) - new and better customer analytics to drive marketing activities and more timely and accurate tracking of marketing campaign effectiveness

Notice how the sentences above don't use the word "Data" at all, or any other data management jargon?

That's because the senior executives who benefit from data management don't care how it's done. They just care about the business outcomes that are relevant to them.

Which CxO stakeholders are benefitting from your Data Management initiative, and how are you making sure you deliver the outcomes they need?

The Need For Clear Data Strategy Outcomes

Why is it so crucial to have a clearly defined outcome for your Data Strategy?

Imagine either:
- You are about to hit a golf ball, OR
- You are about to fire an arrow from a bow

In each case, imagine the hole or target you're aiming for is a very long way away.

What do you do, in order to get the ball or arrow where you want it to go?

Actually, there are going to be lots of things to consider. What's the environment like? Is the weather in your favour or do you need to compensate for high winds? Do you have the right materials (have you chosen the right club in the case of golf, or the right bow and arrow in the case of archery)? How much power do you need to put in, and at what angle?

The first point you may have thought of when I introduced this was obvious and true: if you don't know where you're aiming, you could take the best shot you've ever made, and still completely miss. You could choose the right materials, put in the right level of effort, at the correct angle and elevation, but still be way off the mark.

The second point is: the further away from the target you are, the bigger an impact getting this wrong will have. Even with a clear outcome, if you set yourself up incorrectly and get the angle off just ever so slightly, you will end up much further from the target over a long distance (or long period of time), than if the hole or target is closer.

This is where regularly reviewing progress and making course-corrections can help in a Data programme.

Are you still on track? Is what you are doing working?

Before you continue with the investment and effort that you are expending, do you need to make any adjustments?

Having a clear target is crucial; and then it's important to constantly check that you're on track to hit it, as progress is made in ways that may not have been expected, and the environment changes, and any number of other things result in you inevitably being somewhere slightly different to where you thought you'd be…

Also, is the target still valid or has it moved slightly?

As organisations change, so do priorities; whilst the target may still be in the same broad direction, it's possible that you may need to adapt what you're doing to meet slightly different outcomes.

Had you thought about it this way before? What do you do, to ensure you are heading in the right direction over the long term?

DATA VALUE SUCCESS v1.0

WHY Must Come First!

The "WHY" is everything!

No matter what you are doing, if you are ploughing ahead, driving outputs, but aren't clear on WHY, there is a strong chance that you may be wasting a lot of time and effort on things that aren't going to really help you get to where you need to get to.

This is as true in Data Management as in anything else.

What business outcomes are you trying to drive? How will you measure those business outcomes?

Are you trying to drive new business to increase revenue, or reduce costs, or deliver better customer experiences, or something else?

It's these kinds of real business outcomes that should be the focus - not just outputs or checklist items - so everything you do needs to be designed and delivered in a way that delivers a real impact on them.

Have you clearly defined the business outcomes for your Data Management initiative?

What are you doing to make sure that everything you do aligns to these business outcomes?

Clearly defining the WHY - the business outcomes, tangible benefits and value of any investments - should always be the first step in anything you do.

DATA VALUE SUCCESS v1.0

Succeed Through Execution

THE GAP BETWEEN SUCCESS AND FAILURE in a large data management transformation often isn't just down to the "WHAT", it's down to the "HOW".

The capabilities and processes and structures and things that many data management maturity frameworks and models outline are right and valuable: DAMA DMBOK, EDM Council DCAM, CMMI DMM, and others... they have been written by experts based on real experience and the components are sensible and necessary...

...so if that's the case, why do so many data management initiatives that attempt to implement these frameworks FAIL?

It's the ability to deliver real business value - early, often and continuously - which separates a successful data management initiative from a failed one.

It's also the ability to build the foundations and structures over time, avoiding both the short-term "throw-away" tactical solutions, which deliver immediate value with no enduring capability; as well as avoiding the large-scale (and expensive) "big bang" mega-programmes, which focus too much on theoretical foundations without delivering any real noticeable value.

What are you doing to strike this balance and make your data management initiative successful?

Getting The Flavour Right

What "flavour" of Data Strategy do you need?

And how do you make sure your Data Strategy isn't just a reflection of the preferences of the person writing it?

For example, is the person who is writing your Data Strategy a Master Data Management (MDM) expert, or a Reporting expert, an Advanced Analytics expert, or a Data Quality expert, or something else? I have read many Data Strategies where I could immediately tell the background of the person who wrote it, because they have been written with a strong bias towards a particular perspective.

It's a surprisingly common trap, which even some seasoned data professionals fall into: placing an over-emphasis on the solutions that they are most experienced or most comfortable with, instead of objectively assessing the needs of the business and developing a strategy that delivers relevant and targeted value.

Although most Data Strategies will involve the implementation of many of the same types of data management capabilities, the way in which these capabilities are implemented can vary widely, depending on the business need; and in some cases, some capabilities may be far less important than others, so one Data Strategy can be very different to another.

For example:

If the primary driver for your Data Strategy is to improve the efficiency and reliability of group-level reporting, developing an advanced analytics capability isn't going to be as important as automating the processes and controls around the collection and aggregation of data for group-level reports.

Or...

If the biggest problem your organisation faces is poor customer service due to the poor quality of data, then your Data Strategy is going to need to focus on front-end data capture and operational data quality management (and may also need to involve some operational Master Data Management capabilities, depending on the systems and process architecture).

Whatever solution your Data Strategy specifies, must be aligned to the problems to be addressed and the opportunities to be pursued. The best Data Strategies always start with a very clear definition of the business requirements and a vision for where the organisation wants to get to, along with the benefits to be achieved. The solutions to those problems should then be completely aligned to the realisation of the vision and achievement of the benefits. A well written Data Strategy is balanced and logical in this sense.

Of course, if people contributing to a Data Strategy bring positive experiences of data management solutions that have worked elsewhere, this is going to be a useful and good thing, but it should not be allowed to disproportionally affect the priorities of the strategy, it should only be used to help inform solution options in the context of the outcomes that need to be delivered.

How comfortable are you that your Data Strategy is appropriate and designed to meet your business's needs?

Do You Need To Add A Bit Of Spice?

Is your Data Strategy a bit bland?

Let me guess... you want to monetise your data, reduce costs, drive more revenue, help deliver products to market faster, and reduce risk?...

Um, OK, yep, I can't imagine who wouldn't want to do those things... but aren't they the same generic things that any strategy aims to achieve?

Does your Data Strategy talk about the *specific datasets* that you're going to focus on, or does it just talk about "data" generally?

If it just talks about "data" generally, does it specify *HOW* you will work out which specific datasets you need to address?

Ultimately, the only reason to invest in anything (whether it's Data Management or anything else), is to deliver some kind of value. That value might not be a tangible financial return on investment, but it's got to be something solid (and ideally measurable) enough to justify the investment.

Your Data Strategy should be clear on this from the outset. Everything must start with the business problems or business opportunities, but they need to be specified more clearly than just, for example, "reduce risks": which risks, exactly? And once you know which risks, what data needs to be addressed to reduce these specific risks?

Either asking the question: "what data?"; or "how will we identify the data?" – will take you a step in the right direction. Your Data Strategy doesn't necessarily need to specify the particular datasets that will be in scope, but the more specific you are, the easier it will be to execute and more likely you will be able to deliver the benefits you are aiming to deliver.

How specific is your Data Strategy?

The Importance Of Context And Tailoring

"But why?" I ask again.

I see my colleague's face scrunch up with frustration.

Another round of explanations follow. I am told earnestly that we need metadata, and data owners, and data stewards, and data quality management, and, and...

"Yes, I do agree all of those things are important, but why, in this context? What's the specific problem we're trying to fix with them? And how will we deliver these things in a way that actually fixes the problem?..."

I've had conversations along these lines countless times over the years, often with very capable and experienced data professionals, who I know really do "know their stuff".

Unfortunately, even for a seasoned expert, it can be all too easy to fall into the trap of jumping to a familiar solution, before really understanding the business problem. It is possible to avoid wasted effort and to deliver tangible results through effective data management, but only if your efforts are targeted towards the specific business problem or business opportunity you are aiming at.

I know people are often surprised when I challenge the very practices that I am known for implementing, but it's not the practices I am challenging, it is what we are using them for, to deliver value. I would even go so far as to say that sometimes it's better to do nothing than to invest in data management in the *wrong* way.

Do you recognise this challenge?

Do you always clarify the "why" before deciding on a solution?

What do you do, to make sure you are laser focused on priority business outcomes?

The Best Investments In Data

What does a GREAT investment in Data, Analytics or AI look like?

In my experience, at least two things need to be true:

1. The investment must deliver clear and measurable business benefit, within a reasonable timeframe.

2. The outcome(s) delivered through the investment must be sustainable, not just short term and temporary.

This may seem obvious at face value, but the crucial thing here is that BOTH of these things need to be true, for the investment to be really great - and I have seen far too many Data initiatives that have only been doing one or the other.

This means that purely "foundational", "capability build" investments, on their own, are not great, because they are not tied to specific business benefits, to ensure a meaningful return on investment. (This is a common pitfall of data professionals: focusing on implementing the theoretical things that are needed, missing the link to the tangible business value).

However, it also means that just delivering business benefits that are temporary and do not include any foundational / sustainable capability, are also not a great investment, because the value is limited by its finite, short-term scope. (This is a trap people who don't understand how data management works in practice often fall into - and can initially feel that they've succeeded, until things slip backwards once the data project is closed, or where costs spiral in the future due to technical debt created by poor design decisions).

When it comes to data management, particularly the delivery of cost savings, taking a temporary approach almost always results in the costs that have been seemingly removed, "returning" soon after the work is completed. Tactical investments in data remediation are often a false economy.

What are you doing to make sure your investments in Data, Analytics and AI are GREAT ones?

Move Beyond The Theory

STOP doing things JUST because the data management textbook says so, or because a regulation or law appears to mandate it.

1. WHY are you doing it?
2. What VALUE will it drive?
3. What RISK will it mitigate?

Every so-called 'best practice' in data management was designed for a real purpose, not just for the sake of doing it.

Likewise, every regulation and law that mandates certain data management practices, was designed to drive a positive outcome (no matter how successful or otherwise you may think it has been in doing so - if you look for the intention and the spirit of it, rather than just the "letter of the law", that's where you will find the value).

Re-connect your actions with the underlying purpose and intent, and you will see RADICALLY BETTER RESULTS.

Value And Benefits

Are you writing a data strategy, or a business case for investing in data, analytics and AI?

Looking for ways to frame your challenges and benefits?

How about the following as a really simple set of prompts to help you identify common types of challenges, and the categories of benefits that would come with addressing them?

From → To
CHALLENGE → BENEFIT:

TOO SLOW → FASTER
TOO EXPENSIVE → CHEAPER
NOT GOOD ENOUGH → BETTER
TOO LONG (timeframe) → SHORTER / SOONER
MISSING / NON EXISTANT → NEW
TOO RISKY → SAFER
TOO VAGUE → MORE PRECISE
UNPREDICTABLE → MORE RELIABLE
FAILED → SUCCEEDED
COMPLEX → SIMPLER
MISUNDERSTOOD → UNDERSTOOD / ADOPTED / SUPPORTED / SPONSORED

Hope this helps!

Joining The Dots

One of the great things about enterprise data management is that, done properly, it forces you to join the dots.

It's inevitable, if you approach it in the right way.

The great thing about joining the dots, is that it helps you identify duplication, redundancy and root cause issues, which can result in negative impacts that ripple and multiply across systems and organisational silos.

Fixing those kinds of problems can deliver *significant* value.

It's true that enterprise data management can be challenging, because it involves coordination of lots of people across organisational structures, processes and disparate systems... and that takes top-down empowerment, as well as considerable skill in stakeholder engagement and coordination.

But *not* doing it can be a lot more costly and painful in the long run.

Are you joining the dots?

Plan *AND* Execute To Succeed

"If You Fail to Plan, You Are Planning to Fail." - Benjamin Franklin

"To me, ideas are worth nothing unless executed. They are just a multiplier. Execution is worth millions." - Steve Jobs

How much time and effort should you put into planning vs. execution on your Data initiative?

Execution is critical, but without a clearly defined set of outcomes, you could be travelling very quickly in the wrong direction.

Many data management initiatives involve a lot of activities that can require a lot of people to do a lot of very time consuming things, especially early on when the foundations are being put in place.

This means two things:

1) Execution is key: The longer you wait to start, the further away you will be from achieving your goals (and the task often gets a lot bigger and more costly the longer you leave it, because the volume of data and problems associated with the data and systems and processes can grow significantly)

2) Planning is a pre-requisite: Skipping the plan will almost certainly lead to failure, as you send lots of people off to do lots of things that aren't clearly aligned to your target outcomes and just result in lots of wasted busy work and useless outputs.

Do you have your outcomes for your Data initiative clearly

defined?

How are you making sure your teams are executing their work in a way that delivers to those outcomes?

Effective Is Better Than Exciting

If what you are doing feels a bit "paint by numbers"... a bit dull and basic... then it probably is.

The question is, is what you are doing EFFECTIVE?

If it is effective, then maybe it's OK.

Sometimes the tried-and-tested ways of doing things are the best. That's why they are tried-and-tested!

But if you're like me, you'll want to do more. If you're not delivering a massive, transformational impact, it somehow doesn't feel like it's enough.

And that's a healthy thing, as long as you make sure the basics are done first.

Taking a step back and looking for those great, surprising, out-of-the-box, innovative ideas is a good thing to do. It's how we make progress and improve...

...but if you do some fancy, whizz-bang thing whilst missing the basics, no-one will thank you for it!

Of course, the basics can be delivered in innovative ways too, and you can deliver some transformation in parallel with the basics... but the basics lay the foundations for everything else, and it's always worth remembering that.

The basics take effort and discipline and perseverance to establish and maintain. They are often considered "boring but necessary", and they are absolutely essential.

Do you have that itch to do something new and innovative?

How are you balancing that drive to do things differently, with doing the basics and establishing the foundations first?

Finding The Strategic Impact

If you can't work out what strategic impact you are driving, maybe you need to take a step back.

Then, maybe you need to take even more of a step back.

It is easy to find yourself so close to the day-to-day work, that you lose sight of the bigger picture.

Imagine zooming out, and then zooming out further. Away from the specific data you are dealing with, away from the specific system, the specific team.

Still not finding anything impactful? Zoom back further. To the wider business area, to the company as a whole, to the industry...

At some point you will find things that really matter. Things that are exciting to senior executives, or worrying enough to keep them up at night.

Then you can start tracing back down again. How does the thing you are doing link back to those impactful strategic things?

If they don't at the moment, is there something you could do to adjust them, so that they do?

Or does this exercise reveal that there is something else, which would be far more valuable to focus on?

Even when things seem to be going well, this is a useful exercise to perform.

Real success is found through focusing on the things that drive significant tangible business impact, and sometimes those things can be lost in the mad scramble to "get stuff done" on the immediate priorities and things that seem urgent and important, but may not be when the bigger picture is taken into account.

What are you doing, to make sure you are tying everything you do back to the big strategic things that really matter?

The Best Strategies Consider Logistics

"Amateurs talk strategy. Professionals talk logistics." – General Omar Bradley

"Real strategy lies not in figuring out what to do, but in devising ways to ensure that, compared to others, we actually do more of what everybody knows they should do." – David Maister, Strategy and the Fat Smoker

There is no doubt that strategy is important. Strategy provides clarity about where you are trying to get to, and steps to get there.

One of the most important parts of a strategy is its articulation of WHY you are going to do what you are going to do, and then how you will know when you've got there.

The trouble is, sometimes a strategy can seem a bit obvious. "Surely this is just re-packaged common sense?"

Whilst I do think it is important to seek opportunities to do things differently, and in data management there are plenty of opportunities to leverage technologies in new and innovative ways, it's also important to remember that "dull but effective" steps should not be discarded just because they are not seen to be innovative enough.

A strategy doesn't need to be innovative, to be the right thing to do.

Often, amazing outcomes are achieved through amazing execution, not through revolutionary ideas.

Execution can also be the hardest bit, and where real

experience comes into play.

A strategy may say something that sounds like common sense at a high level, but do you really know *how* you are going to get it done?

Beneath the high-level chevrons on your grand strategic roadmap, there will always be a stack of detail to actually make it happen.

And it is the detail – the LOGISTICS – the specifics about how to get these things done – especially in large, complex organisations – which will make all the difference between success and failure.

"Professionals talk logistics." I would have to agree.

Do you talk strategy or logistics?

Don't Miss The Point

Are you missing the point with your Data Strategy?

It's true that a core purpose of a Data Strategy is to clearly define how a business outcome, or set of business outcomes, will be achieved, BUT...

...there is also REAL VALUE in using it to obtain and sustain buy-in from key stakeholders.

Focus on business outcomes that RESONATE with your key business stakeholders, to unlock the value!

THINK:

WHO matters most? Is it your CEO, COO, or some other stakeholders?

WHY should THEY care?

HOW will your strategy help THEM achieve THEIR desired outcomes?

Remember: no matter what you're doing, always put the value first.

What are you doing, to deliver a value-first Data Strategy?

A Story About Getting It Wrong

The table of contents of the latest Data Strategy looked perfect... and yet, something wasn't quite right...

It seemed to have everything: a vision; a set of target outcomes and success measures; a delivery framework, with roles and responsibilities; a set of deliverables and milestones; a roadmap; and a load of supporting appendices.

But in the review session with the first of the senior stakeholders who were going to be signing it off, it was clear something was wrong.

The senior manager frowned and they seemed to stiffen up, shifting in their chair uncomfortably.

"I'm sorry, this is the first time I've seen this, you'll just have to give me a minute..."

Your heart sank as you realised mistake number one: you hadn't engaged with your stakeholders until now, and had just presented it to them as a "done deal".

The thing is, you know that it doesn't matter if your strategy is perfect or not: if your stakeholders feel like they are being pressured into making a decision on something, which they haven't had any input into, you may have set yourself up to fail before you even start.

There's a little cough, and a raised finger: "Um... what does 'Automated metadata harvesting' mean, and how does it help deliver any reduction in costs?"

Oh. Yeah. And you left all the Data Management jargon in there, too, but didn't explain how these theoretical things would deliver the desired impact.

If you want to deliver a successful Data Strategy, you need to involve key people in the process of writing it, and you need to make it all about the delivery of business outcomes.

In many cases, you can completely avoid a lot of Data jargon, which may be important for how things will be delivered, behind the scenes, but many of the people who need to read the Strategy, won't need to know about that level of detail.

What will you do, to avoid this kind of scenario happening for you?

Part 3:
Data Leadership

Why You Need Great Data Leadership

Your Data Leadership team is *THE* KEY to making your Data initiative successful.

Of course, you will need great "doers" in your Data team – they're the people who will "get the job done", at the end of the day – but a great team, without great leadership, is still set up to fail.

The greater the scale of your initiative, the more important this becomes.

Great leaders are crucial for setting direction, for leading day-to-day, and for both recruiting, and for coaching and developing a high performing team.

This does of course all start with the "one at the top".

Who is the person, who will shape and lead the team overall?

The right person to lead a Data team can vary widely based on the outcomes that an organisation is trying to deliver, the scale of the company, and the specific responsibilities of the role.

This is why the selection of the right leader needs to be done carefully.

It really is worth putting the effort into defining the OUTCOMES of roles clearly, and putting in the TIME to find the right person.

Better to take a long time and find the right person, than rush the process and put your entire strategy at risk.

DATA VALUE SUCCESS v1.0

Are you clear on the outcomes your organisation is trying to drive, and the specific type of leader you will need to make your strategy successful?

How To Find The RIGHT Data Leader

The steps for recruiting the best Data leadership for your organisation are simple, in principle.

So why do so many companies get it so wrong?!

At a high level, the steps are:

1. Work out what outcomes you want to deliver

2. Work out the skillsets needed to deliver those outcomes

3. Define the leadership role (or roles) needed to create and lead the team to deliver those outcomes (create a job spec)

4. Perform a search for the people you need (using the channels and partner organisations that will best help you find those people)

5. Engage with the best candidates, to make sure they are right for you and to help them make sure your company is right for them too (in other words, run an interviewing process)

6. Offer a package that is appropriate for the role and the calibre of person you need

And yet, no matter how simple these steps appear, it is shockingly common how often steps are either poorly executed, or skipped altogether!

> If you don't know what outcomes you're going to deliver, you have no way of working out what skillsets and experience you need.

> If you don't know what skillsets you need, you can't possibly define the role or roles you need to deliver the outcomes.

> If you can't define the roles you need, any search you do will lack direction and identify the wrong people.

> And after all that, even if you are lucky enough to find the right people, if you don't engage with them in the right way and don't offer them an appropriate package, you're not going to be able to get them to join you anyway!

This is no different to any other recruitment exercise, and every step deserves care and attention, to get it right.

But what should you look for in a great DATA Leader, specifically?

A great Data Leader needs:

- Great leadership skills and soft skills for engaging and positively influencing people

- Rounded Data Management skills - at a minimum, an appreciation of the full data delivery lifecycle and concepts from data quality to data analytics

- Technical skills that are particularly relevant to your organisation and to the role, taking into account their seniority and what they will actually be doing. (A super senior global leader may not need to write any code; the hands-on leader of a technical delivery team may need to be an expert programmer)

Remember that tailoring to your organisation is a critical success factor here!

Of course, the state of the job market and a variety of

other factors will undeniably have an impact on your ability to recruit; but if you are really clear on your requirement and follow ALL of these steps, with support from recruiters with the right market knowledge and approach, you will stand a far better chance of finding the person or people you need.

Are you looking for a Data leader?

What are you doing, to make sure you find the BEST person or people, to meet your company's needs?

The Feeling Of Great Data Leadership

What does great Data leadership feel like?

Have you ever experienced this before?...

...From Day 1, it was obvious that the newly appointed Data Leader was the right person for the job.

They immediately engaged with senior leaders across the organisation, to understand their needs. Every person they met was impressed by the way they listened and demonstrated both their understanding and their ability to offer options for ways forwards.

They engaged with their new team, to understand what was working and not working; to assess skills and aspirations; and to establish management structures for effective communication, with clear prioritisation and direction.

They had just the right level of technical capability to lead, balanced with people leadership and stakeholder engagement skills.

Within weeks, everyone could "feel" the difference.

There was a clarity of VISION. Everyone knew where they were going.

There was clarity about PRIORITIES and PROGRESS. Everyone knew where they were and what was being delivered.

Some things were STOPPED; other things were STARTED; and every change in direction was directly aligned to a very clear set of target BUSINESS OUTCOMES.

There was also a renewed sense of AMBITION; a belief in the ART OF THE POSSIBLE; balanced with a strong sense of PRAGMATISM and DRIVE FOR SUSTAINABLE RESULTS.

Of course, the real test would be the delivery of results in the medium-to-long term... but after various previous failed attempts at delivering Data and Analytics capabilities, this time it felt... different.

For the first time in a long time, there was HOPE...

THIS is what great Data leadership feels like.

Leadership Skills Are Key

Are you missing the point with your attempts to establish the right Data Leadership?

It's true that it's important to find people with the right technical skills, BUT...

...there is REAL VALUE in leaders who can effectively engage, inspire and LEAD.

Focus on finding people who are right for delivering the change YOUR organisation needs right now, really taking into consideration your organisation's specific culture and current situation, to unlock the value!

WHY do you need leadership at the moment? What BUSINESS OUTCOMES do you need to deliver, and what kind of person would be best suited to lead the delivery of those outcomes?

Do you need someone to lead a small tech team, or someone to deliver a large-scale organisational transformation?

There's a big difference in the type of person needed for each of these things!

For some leadership roles, having deep Python, SQL, Java or other technical experience may be essential. For others, it may be totally irrelevant.

WHO is your leader going to be leading, and WHO will they need to engage with and influence?

HOW are they going to need to land and engage with your organisation?

DATA VALUE SUCCESS v1.0

No matter what you're doing, always put the value first.

What are you doing, to put value first when establishing Data Leadership?

Top Tip For Any Data Leader

Would you like to know a simple trick to quickly improve the effectiveness of your Data & Analytics function?

This is not always easy to do, but I can guarantee that it works, if you really commit to doing it (and it works in other aspects of business and in life too, if you want to give it a go):

STEP 1: Ask yourself the question: if there was ONE THING that I could STOP, or GET OUT OF, with the gift of hindsight, what would that be?

STEP 2: STOP IT, or GET OUT OF IT, as quickly as possible.

And that's it!

(You can of course make a list of things you want to stop rather than just identifying one thing - but it's always a good idea to identify a priority and focus on it until it's done, before moving onto anything else).

That might sound easy, but often it isn't.

I bet you could think of a few things you would stop now if you had the choice, so why are you still doing them? Maybe stopping them just doesn't seem like a priority? Or the effort involved seems too much to make it worthwhile?

It might be time to re-think. The act of stopping things that are driving cost and waste is almost always worth investing time into. It's amazing how it can create space for so much more productivity and success, sometimes without even needing to start anything new.

A common example I've seen, is where a new data platform has been in "development hell" for a long time, has received a lot of financial investment but is either not delivering or is driving more problems than it solves; but where senior management are resistant to cut their losses and do something different, despite the spiralling costs. The fear of "losing face" is very real and can drive some pretty dysfunctional behaviour.

Another common one is where a process has been implemented, where your team has committed to someone (such as a regulator or some senior stakeholder), that it would be done, but in practice it's a massive drain on time and not adding value. Stopping it will take some explaining and you will face resistance – but the minute you do, you will free up all of that time and wasted energy to focus on other things.

Or it could be something even more challenging, like a third party contract which you would not have got into if you had known how it was going to pan out; or a person in your team who just isn't performing.

Each of these things may be difficult to admit, and even more difficult to resolve – but it's an amazingly fast and effective way to drive improvements, if you are honest about the problem and tackle it head-on.

The impact of costly, wasted effort, is far broader than just the time and energy spent on that wasted thing. It often has a knock-on impact to various other things.

When was the last time you considered what you would STOP, to be able to GO FASTER?

De-Risking A Data Programme

How do you de-risk your Data Transformation programme?

Here are a few key things to maximise your chances of success:

1. Establish the right leadership and expertise. Get this right, and the leaders will make sure the other critical success factors are dealt with!

1. However, just in case you haven't quite nailed the leadership, you also need to...

2. Really clearly define the business outcomes / benefits you are aiming to deliver (NOT "data management capabilities"- I mean actual measurable improvements or financial benefits)

3. Break the work into discrete chunks, to enable the delivery of incremental value in reasonable timescales i.e. days, weeks and months - not years!

4. Deliver foundational capability that is sustainable and based on good practice, at the same time as delivering the discrete chunks of benefits.

5. Did I mention getting the right people on the team?

6. Of course, a data transformation initiative is also just like any other change programme, so applying good project management / delivery management practices will also help (which will include risks and issues management, for example)...

What do you do to de-risk your Data initiative?

The Perils Of Mis-Selling A Data Role

"I quit."

Jaws dropped. There was stunned silence.

"But you've only been here two months! WHY?!"

The fact that anyone was even asking this question was yet more evidence that the decision to resign was the right one.

Put simply, what had been promised was completely different to the reality; and no-one had any idea just how far off they were.

The vision that had been sold was one of strategic transformation; the reality was a tactical turnaround of an underperforming and under-resourced MI team.

The promise had been top-down sponsorship and investment; the reality was a shoestring budget and a total lack of appreciation for what it would take to make anything work.

The reality was, even if they got what they really needed – which was a technical team leader for the MI team, to tactically improve their performance, not an executive-level Chief Data Officer – they still weren't going to succeed, because there was none of the support needed.

The MI team were getting hammered for not delivering, but were being given none of the support they needed to turn things around.

Every suggestion to improve was rejected, with the response being that the team just needed to work harder.

But no-one could see it. More importantly, the leaders of the company were unwilling to see it, even if others could.

So with that, they lost their newly appointed Chief Data Officer, not long after they had joined.

After all the time, cost and effort that was put into recruiting them, it turned out that the appointment was doomed to fail long before they had recruited them – because they had never really been committed to the changes needed to succeed, in the first place.

They had sold a false vision to someone, to get them to join.

Maybe they could have succeeded if the vision was real, but without the commitment from the top, it was never going to work.

At the end of the day, there's no point in hiring a senior Data leader, if you're not committed to setting them up for success.

The Importance Of A Great Data Team

Is there anything more important than building a GREAT Data team?

You could remove the word "data" from the sentence above, and it would hold true for anything you are trying to do.

Great leadership. The right mix of roles, skillsets, and experiences. More importantly than skills, the right attitudes and work ethic.

If you want to deliver anything at scale, you can't do it alone.

The famous African proverb wisely states: "If you want to go fast, go alone. If you want to go far, go together."

In my experience, a great team, who have worked together for long enough to gel and to know how to make the best of each other's strengths and weaknesses, can not only go far, but they can do it at an ever-increasing pace too.

How do you make sure you have the right capability and capacity to achieve your goals?

Of course, you need to be clear on what you are trying to do, in order to determine the products and services you want to deliver, and then to design the team you need to deliver those outcomes.

But team design alone is useless if you don't get the right people together, and if you don't organise and lead them in the right way.

Great people with a poor org design will self-organise and succeed. The wrong people recruited into a perfectly designed org structure will flounder and fail.

What do you do to attract, retain, and get the most out of the best people for the job?

Data & Analytics Operating Model

Designing a Data Management & Analytics operating model is NEVER a one-size-fits all exercise.

Standard org design structures, maturity frameworks and functional models can all be helpful to make sure you've been conscious about what's in and out of scope, but trying to implement these reference models "as they are" never works.

It is absolutely crucial that you clearly define the outcomes your organisation is going to deliver, and who the internal and external customers of those outcomes are, to be able to define how your organisation needs to be structured and how it will operate.

Whether you centralise or federate, or have a hybrid model; and whether you have functional or cross-functional teams; and how the various teams interact and operate, is all context-specific and needs to be designed around a range of factors including the outcomes they will deliver, as well as the broader structure and culture of your specific organisation.

And if you are re-designing an existing operating model, a key step is to understand what is and isn't currently working. Even if some of the bits that are currently working are not going to be part of the target state, don't throw them away yet!

Success breeds success: keep the things that currently work and use them as part of your new foundation to build on first!

There are methodologies for operating model design, which I absolutely do recommend you use, because they have been developed in a way that will increase your chances of success.

But the reality is, doing this properly takes real-world experience. It's only possible to pick up so much from methodologies, books and training; but at the end of the day, nothing beats seeing several different org structures in the real world and learning what works or doesn't, in practice.

What are your experiences of Chief Data Office / Data & Analytics organisation structures? What have you seen work and what have you seen fail? What are you doing to apply these lessons today?

Part 4: Data Accountabilities

Why Data Accountabilities?

If you want to get anything done, at any kind of scale, you need to be clear on who is going to do what.

This is just a simple fact, which applies to anything – not just Data-related things.

And in a Data Management context, especially in a large organisation, being really clear on who is accountable for what, is a crucial step in setting your initiative up for success.

When looking at Data Management holistically, there are almost always people in other parts of the business, who will play an important role.

For example:

- Who captures Data?

- Who looks after the systems that capture and process the Data?

- Who uses the Data?

- Who leads the teams of people, who capture and use the Data?

...and so on...

Whether you decide to assign these people to roles, such as "Data Producer" and "Systems Owner", or decide not to; knowing who these people are, and being clear with them about what their responsibilities are, will dramatically improve your ability to deliver your Data initiative.

The trick is to establish these accountabilities, in a way that enables you to deliver faster and more effectively (NOT as an administrative exercise that just wastes people's time).

Before you assign any roles, you need to start by working out what outcomes you are aiming to drive.

Then you need to work out: who will need to play a role in helping you achieve these outcomes?

Who will need to DO things?

Who will need to FUND things or PRIORITISE things for their teams to DO?

Who will need to DECIDE or APPROVE things?

Who will need to INFLUENCE things, and HOW?

Make this a really tangible exercise first, thinking about real people doing real things, and how it will work in practice.

Make sure you write down the really specific ACTIONS that people will need to perform, not just fluffy generalised statements.

Then, when you apply labels to these roles, you can do so with really concrete examples, in a way that helps people understand what they need to do, and how their actions will complement and interact with other people's actions.

Doing it this way, role labels can actually become a useful communication tool, rather than yet another layer of jargon and admin.

DATA VALUE SUCCESS v1.0

Always remember that this is all about making sure things happen in the right way, not about making sure there's paperwork to make it look like you know what you're doing.

Where To Start With Data Accountabilities & Responsibilities

Data Accountabilities are important – but what are they all about, in practice?

First, just to be clear: we ARE talking about assigning people to roles, here.

Which is often not the most popular thing to do.

People don't like being given more responsibilities, "on top of their day jobs", so we need to go into this with open eyes, and be really clear about WHY we are doing this, for it to work.

Because this is about identifying people who need to be DOING things. It's not just about putting people's names in boxes for the sake of it, it's about delivering change.

So how do we do this, in a "Value-First" way?

There are several parts to this, but it all starts, as with everything else: with the OUTCOMES that you are looking to drive.

You should only be assigning people to roles where they are really needed, to drive value, or support the delivery of value, somehow.

DON'T just blindly assign loads of people to roles like "Data Owner" and things, for the sake of it. You will be setting yourself up for failure by doing this.

Second, link people's roles to really specific actions and real value. If people can see the point, they are far more likely to engage, than if it just looks like a theoretical waste of time.

The other really important thing that comes along with this, is you need to empower people to do the things you are asking them to do. Do they have the guidance and tools to fulfil their responsibilities?

If not, you are setting them up for fail, and yourself up to fail, too.

Next – and this is the most powerful tip – where possible, make the "roles" part of people's existing roles, not "new" things to do "on top of their day jobs".

In many cases, what you will actually be doing, is just clarifying what people are ALREADY doing, or clarifying what they *SHOULD* have been doing anyway, even if they didn't realise it!

Most Data-related roles are not new roles at all, they are just good practice.

If you need to roll things out at scale, I would still recommend phasing the rollout of *responsibilities*, aligned to when people need to do things. If you assign people to roles, then they don't need to do anything for ages, they're probably going to forget and disengage by the time you actually do need them to do something.

If you don't have people on the hook to do things in the business, you will struggle to delivery your Data Initiative; but it's crucial that you put Value first, and only assign accountabilities in a way that is practical and supports the delivery of business outcomes.

Are you trying to assign Data accountabilities? How are you making sure that you do this in a Value-first way?

The Fear Of New Data Roles

Do you have any data-specific roles in place, in your organisation?

Do they help, or just cause more complexity and confusion?

For busy people who aren't data experts, being assigned to a new "data role" can be a scary thing.

What extra things am I being signed up to? Will I have the time and resources to fulfil the new responsibilities? Is it going to be worth it or just a load of extra side of desk work with no real benefit for me?

And these are valid fears. I've seen many examples where data management roles are broad and vague and not set up for success, leading to stress and wasted effort and failure and disappointment.

Creating clarity about exactly what people need to do, how and why, can be extremely powerful- and in many cases essential.

Targeted, thoughtful and well implemented new roles can be an important part of making this work.

But badly implemented new roles can create more problems than good...

What is your organisation doing to make sure data management responsibilities are clear, and rolled out in an effective way?

Getting Accountability Frameworks Wrong

If an Accountability framework creates division and silos, the way it's been implemented is wrong.

Whilst clarification of accountabilities and responsibilities is vital, especially where there is a need for segregation of duties, there should be more of a focus on the interactions needed between people in these roles to achieve outcomes.

RACI matrices are an important tool in process design, but here's the important point: they are used to clarify who does what in the context of the delivery of an end-to-end process. Each step is dependent on each other and consequently each role is dependent on one another.

The minute you hear people using their accountabilities as an excuse to avoid collaboration ("that's not my accountability", "that's not in scope for me", etc) – it's possible that something's not quite right. This applies to all types of roles: business, technology, change, data…

There is no doubt that formalised accountability is important and needed.

But do those who are accountable understand that they are dependent on others, and just as they need others to collaborate with them, they need to be doing the same for everyone to collectively succeed?

The Universal Facts About How Data Responsibilities Work, In All Organisations

The following pages are taken from an article that I published, which presents a different and simpler spin on how responsibilities for data work in most organisations, plus a few pointers for things companies can do to make data management roles even more effective.

It's a bit longer than the other posts included in this book, but I've received really positive feedback on it, so thought it would be useful to include in full.

The wonderful truth: establishing who is responsible for data is easy!

It's really common for organisations to struggle with concepts such as "data ownership", "data stewardship", "data custodianship" and the like. When these ideas are introduced, they are often met with resistance, especially when they are communicated as something "new" that need to be done in addition to people's "day jobs".

The great thing is, working out who is responsible for data is extremely simple and is based on the fundamental way that any organisation works. "Data ownership" and related concepts make a lot more sense when they are understood in the context of established foundations of responsibility for data.

Even better than this is the fact that the basic responsibilities of anyone in relation to data are universally the same in all organisations. The way it works is so amazingly straightforward, in some ways it's astounding that the basic facts that apply to every company, anywhere in the world, are not more widely recognised.

So, in this article, I'm going to provide a very simple and clear explanation of how responsibility for data works in any organisation, including a brief overview of some common ownership structures and how the data roles (owner, steward, custodian) can fit with the way that any organisation operates.

Starting at the bottom

When dealing at an individual level, responsibility for data is obvious. Let's say we're dealing with someone working in a call centre or in a shop or some other role that involves capturing data. They may have a hard copy paper form that they're filling in, or may be typing data directly into a system.

Whoever they are, they are responsible for capturing the data that they capture. If they decide not to fill in one of the mandatory fields, that's up to them. If they mis-spell something, that's not anyone else's fault.

Just think about this scenario for a moment. There's no-one else who could possibly be held responsible for what they decide to do. The organisation that they work for may be able to provide them with better systems or forms, with validation that doesn't allow them to make some mistakes, and may provide them with more training and support; but ultimately, when it comes down to the action of capturing the data, it's their responsibility.

Expanding that out for a moment, the way in which they handle the data is their responsibility too. If they decide to take a copy out of the office and leave it somewhere insecure, or to send it to someone who shouldn't have access to it, they are responsible for that.

What about if they are given data by someone else?

Maybe they've received a partially complete form and are using the data that they have been given to perform some calculations and are capturing more data in the rest of the form. Are they responsible for the data that they received?

No, clearly not. The person who captured the data before them was responsible for it when they captured it. However, from the point that someone receives data, they become responsible for what they do with it. If they spot that the data is inaccurate, then they can either choose to take that into consideration (and either contact the person they received it from, or log and escalate the issue, or seek to correct it somehow); or could decide to knowingly use the data, despite the fact that it's wrong. That decision is their responsibility.

This leads to a similar question: what about when they pass the data onto someone else?

At the point that they pass the data onto someone else, their decision to pass it on, who they are passing it onto and whether or not they notify the person (or system, or process, or whatever) that they are passing it onto of the shortcomings in the data, is up to them. It's their responsibility. Also, if there are specific ways in which the data should or should not be used, it's up to them to make that clear when they're passing it on.

Once the data is passed on somewhere else, it's no longer in their control. They cannot be held responsible for things that they don't do to the data, but they absolutely are responsible for everything that they did with the data when they had it, including capturing it, editing it, processing it, storing it, transferring it, deleting it, or passing it onto someone else.

So, we have now established the basic facts of data responsibilities at the lowest level. In summary, if you capture or process data, you are responsible for it while it is in your possession. Time to move up a level...

One level up

If you run a team, you are responsible for the conduct and performance of the individuals in your team. This is a universal truth in most organisations following a standard management structure.

As such, a team leader is responsible for the data that their team captures and processes. If the team doesn't capture data they are supposed to, or captures invalid, inaccurate data, or mishandles it resulting in security breaches due to the actions that they have taken, the team leader is responsible, just as the individual in their team is responsible for their actions.

Can you see where this is going?

Rolling up and up

This same concept of responsibility for data rolls up an organisation. If you run a group of teams, you are responsible for all the data that your teams create and process.

If you run a division or business unit or function in a company, you are responsible for all the data that your part of the company processes.

All this responsibility rolls up and up until it reaches the head of the company: the CEO, MD or whoever runs the organisation.

So, there you have it: super simple and totally aligned to how any organisations works.

Simple yet effective

Some people may now be wondering what the big deal is: isn't what I've just described obvious?

On the one hand, yes, it is. The thing is, when an organisation attempts to put in place more sophisticated and formalised data governance arrangements, there is a risk that the obvious truths outlined above are lost in translation. No matter what data management structures are implemented, the above will always be true; moreover, the fundamental responsibilities are really important, because they are the foundations upon which any formalised structures will need to operate.

Building on these basic ideas, I'll now step through several other, more "formalised" roles, which can each play an important part when implementing a set of well-rounded data management arrangements. The first couple of roles are not always considered to be "core" data management roles but are often necessary and have the potential to be extremely powerful and useful. In the sections that follow, I'll also cover some of the classic data roles associated with data governance, to explain how these fit into the simple model of responsibilities that I have already outlined.

Business System ownership: an important and powerful role

Now that the basic and universally true concept of responsibility for data has been established, and before I get onto "Data Owners" and the like, I'd like to make a little detour to a role that is often mis-implemented and massively underrated when trying to manage data effectively.

Let's start with another obvious fact: systems* contain data. Data does not exist unless it is stored or processed somewhere, and no matter what amazing data ownership framework you come up with, your actual data will be stored in systems.

(* Note for techies and architects: I'm using the term "system" loosely and broadly to mean any kind of technology that data can be represented in, in some way, whether it be an application, database, data object, or whatever.)

As a result, if you want to do something to a system, such as implement a change to it or get access to it to change the data within it or something like that, you need someone that you can get to complete that action. In large organisations, where there are lots of systems and lots of competing priorities and budgetary constraints, it's particularly important to have someone who can be held accountable for each system.

However, the person needs to be in a position where they care about the system and have budget to be able to make changes if necessary. This person generally shouldn't be someone in IT who runs the system on behalf of someone in the business and who is therefore just there to keep the lights on and has no vested interest in its effective operation. It also can't be someone in the business who is only responsible for day-to-day operations but has no budgetary responsibility.

It's common for "system ownership" to be established but for it to be ineffective because the wrong person has been appointed. This isn't a sign that system ownership isn't worth establishing, it's a sign that the wrong person has been identified as Business System Owner. Often, the right Business System Owner is relatively senior and often runs the teams of people who are the main or only users of a system (although this is not always the case).

Why the detour to system ownership?

First, because if you assign the correct Business System Owners, when you assign Data Owners, and when you also combine this with the formalisation of the fundamental responsibilities for data that I outlined previously, the Data Owners will then be able to leverage these other roles to be effective in fulfilling their obligations. Without these other roles and responsibilities being formalised, Data Owners' jobs become a lot harder or in some cases virtually impossible, meaning that their success will then be totally dependent on the talents and experience of the individuals appointed into their roles rather than through organisational empowerment.

Second, there's the opportunity to supercharge the system owner role. This is where you can take a System Owner from being a key supporter, to being an absolute cornerstone in your data management strategy.

How?

By making Business System Owners responsible for the governance of the data in their systems. What does this mean? It means making them responsible for knowing what data is coming into and going out of their system; for checking the quality of data as it's fed into their system from elsewhere and flagging when it's poor quality; for putting in place validation rules so that people can't directly input invalid data and for reporting on the quality of the data in their systems; and for putting in place mechanisms to secure the data in their systems and to manage the transfer of data to anyone else or to any other systems, including establishment of data sharing agreements before datasets are transferred downstream.

If you make this shift, it really transforms the role. It

means there's someone who cares about establishing these mechanisms for maintaining the data, who should take pro-active action to do so, and can be held to account if they don't. This is a step that many organisations do not make and it is true that you can establish data management arrangements that work without it, but I can assure you that when this kind of clear set of responsibilities is established, it can result in a step-change.

Notice for a moment the similarities in this supercharged Business System Owner's role and the role of an individual in relation to data. It's very similar. A Business System Owner can be responsible for governing the data that's in their system, for making sure that users of their system follow their rules, and that they control the flow of out of their system. They cannot however be responsible for the data that is passed into their system and can only be responsible for the data when it's passed out insofar as a data sharing agreement is put in place.

Also notice that a Business System Owner is not directly responsible for the data itself, within their system, unless they also run the teams of people who capture and process the data in their system. They absolutely can govern the way that the data in the system is captured and processed, for example by implementing validation and data quality rules, but they can only be responsible for the things that are in their control. This aligns to the facts established before.

Process Owners - for completeness...

Given that I've touched on Business System Owners, I thought it was important to address the concept of "process ownership" too, especially for organisations that already have such a role in place. Moreover, even if you only have the concept of localised process ownership, if you consider that a process has a set of inputs, which will include data inputs; that a process then performs a set of tasks, which almost always involves processing data; and then a process delivers some outputs, which often also involve data... I hope that you will have already spotted the pattern of responsibility that an organisation has an opportunity to follow and leverage.

A Process Owner is an individual that has been assigned as accountable for an end-to-end process, which may often span multiple organisational siloes. In a simplistic data management model, having Process Owners in place is useful to have someone to go to in order to implement changes to a process where that process is driving problems. For example, if it's identified that a particular step in a process is driving poor quality data, then there is an individual who is accountable for that process and has the resources to make changes and rectify the process step in order to resolve the problem.

However, just as with Business System Owners, if you take the role of Process Owner a step further and also make them responsible for the way in which data is managed throughout their process; with the same constraints as those that apply at an individual level i.e. they are responsible for capture and processing within their process, and for the way data is passed onto other processes (including clarity on how the data should be used by downstream processes), but not for data that they receive as inputs, which they have a responsibility to push back and log issues with... this type of ownership also becomes complementary and very powerful.

I hope that this concept of responsibility for data, which applies at an individual level, team level, organisational level, and within the span of control of roles such as Business System Owner and Process Owner, is starting to become clearer as you think about each of these roles in the same way. This way of thinking also naturally aligns to the next two roles that I am about to introduce.

Data Producers and Data Consumers

I've nearly got to data ownership roles, but before I get there, it's worth making a general point that all of the responsibilities that I have described so far, are variations on Data Producer roles (i.e. if you're the producer of data, you are responsible for its production) and Data Consumer roles (i.e. if you consume data, you have a set of requirements for what you want to consume and must use it in line with the purpose for which the data was originally created).

At a basic level, anyone who captures or processes data is responsible for how they capture or process it. Most people are both producers and consumers of data at some stage or other, and when producing or consuming data, are responsible for the way in which they do so. The same concepts apply to Business System Owners and Process Owners, and these all offer opportunities to formalise roles across your organisation to deliver a far more powerful network of responsibilities supporting good data management practices.

However, the roles and responsibilities that have been outlined so far, on their own, don't quite provide the kind of robust, end-to-end "data ownership" that is often required for enterprise-wide data management to really work. Also, whilst these roles and responsibilities may seem to overlap, if implemented properly any overlap is totally complementary and will not be duplicative at all, because it leads to constructive collaboration between roles to accelerate to better ways of work. Each role is an important enabler for all others, which can make a huge difference to the effectiveness of data management practices across an organisation.

Why do you need data ownership, when you've established all these other responsibilities and things?

Whilst everything I've explained in the sections above is useful and important to manage data effectively, in most organisations, especially large ones, the problems encountered with data are not found at an individual system or process level. Instead, they manifest themselves in inconsistencies across multiple systems; or in the misuse of data in scenarios that the data was not originally captured for. For example, if the same data in three systems, is captured in different ways (for example using different formats and structures), when they feed into a central system, they will clash and cause all kinds of operational and analytical issues. Likewise, if data is captured for one purpose and then used for something totally different, it could not only result in the wrong outcomes but could also be directly breaking several laws and regulations at the same time!

As a result, one of the critical things that most data management initiatives tackle is cross-system and cross-process alignment, consistency and harmonisation. Whilst good data management practices are absolutely critical at an individual system and individual process level too, the most common need for "data ownership" is found in the need for common data rules and data governance across multiple systems.

As such, a "Data Owner" is usually established to address this point.

Depending on the data management model that you are following, there are two types of "Data Owner".

The first type of Data Owner is the owner of a particular

"data set". This owner is accountable for the content in a data set, for example the official master records of a set of customers, held in a master data source. The responsibilities of this type of Data Owner very clearly follows the responsibilities described above; however, their responsibilities can be enhanced in relation to governance of the use of their data, with powers to both establish "data sharing agreements" before any data consumers can access the data that they own, and with enforcement powers to remove access and escalate where they find that their data is being mis-used.

In some organisations, the owner of a data set may also be the owner of the system that contains the data and the processes that capture and use the data. Following the lines of responsibilities lined out in this series of posts, it is usually quite straightforward to work out who this person is and it is usually this person who will most care about the way in which the data is handled, because they are often responsible for both the value driven in the use of the data and the consequences if something were to go wrong with it.

The second type of Data Owner is often referred to as a "Data Domain Owner", and is responsible for setting the common rules that are followed for a particular set of data that they are responsible for, and for running the governance arrangements that oversee conformance to those rules.

For example, a Data Domain Owner may be appointed for the "Customer" data domain, with responsibility for setting the rules for how Customer data is captured and processed; and then for engaging with the relevant Business System Owners, Process Owners and organisational leaders to ensure that data is only captured and processed in accordance with the standard rules.

As a result, a "Data Domain Owner" can only be directly responsible for data that is created by them or their teams; so in most cases, a "Data Domain Owner" is reliant on other individuals in roles across the organisations to fulfil their obligations, which further explains the importance of establishing the other data responsibilities and system ownership roles.

In some cases, where an authoritative, master source of data has been established, the "Data Set Owner" for the data in the master source may also be appointed as the "Data Domain Owner" for that data as it exists across the organisation, which can significantly increase the empowerment of the individual to drive consistent data management practices for the data that they "own". For example, the Customer data managed in a Master Data Management platform may be assigned to someone as both Data Set Owner and Data Domain Owner for Customer data. This means that they are both able to directly control the data within the platform (within the bounds of the data responsibilities explained in previous parts of this series of posts) and may also set the wider rules and governance for Customer data as it is captured, stored and processed elsewhere across their organisation.

At this point, you will see why it's easy for data management responsibilities to appear to be quite jargon-heavy and complicated, but they really aren't as complicated as they appear. If you keep going back to the basic concepts of responsibilities that were introduced in the first few sections of this article, the same principles apply. No matter what role you are fulfilling, you can be responsible for data when it's in your possession but not when it's not. You can be responsible for governance of data that others use, but your empowerment will be dependent on other roles and structures in your organisation to enable you to discharge your governance responsibilities effectively.

Now I've covered "Data Owner" roles ("Dataset owners" and "Data Domain Owners"), I'll move onto two other common Data Management roles: "Data Custodians" and "Data Stewards".

Data Custodians – looking after the containers of data

I tend to think of Data Custodians as anyone who looks after a "container" of data but who doesn't touch the data in it themselves (unless specifically instructed as a technical action, rather than as a day-to-day responsibility). By "container", I mean anything that stores data, such as a system or network folder or filing cabinet or anything else that holds data, either temporarily or longer-term.

A Data Custodian looks after data indirectly, but they are not directly responsible for its quality or security, beyond the operation of the processes and controls that are in place on the container i.e. they are an "owner" of the container, not of the contents of the container.

For example, a System Owner is generally a considered to be a Data Custodian (unless their role is beefed up to be more than this and to cover direct responsibility for the data within their system, in line with some of the ideas at the beginning of this article). They manage the system and make sure the relevant mechanisms are in place to maintain the data within it, but do not touch the data or play any role in setting the rules in relation to the data.

Data Stewards – a broad term!

The term "Data Steward" is used broadly and often quite differently in different organisations. It is also sometimes used inter-changeably with terms such as "Data Champion", "Data Curator", "Data Keeper", "Data Trustee" and various others; which is why it's important that each role in a data management organisation is clearly defined to avoid confusion. A Data Steward in one organisation may be very different to another.

So, for the purposes of this post, I'm going to introduce two type of Data Steward that are useful to support a Data Domain Owner in fulfilling their obligations. The term "steward" is chosen due to the idea of someone who "looks after" the data; they care about it and play a role in maintaining it, even if in some cases in a governance position.

Data Stewards are the rule-setters and guardians of data.

The first type of Data Steward, which we could call a "Domain Data Steward", usually reports into a Data Domain Owner, with responsibility for engaging across business areas in relation to their particular Data Domain, for example Customer or Product. Where a data management structure has been implemented around "Data Domains", a Data Domain Owner is accountable for governing their Data Domain and any Data Stewards that they have working for them are responsible for the fulfilment of their accountabilities.

The second type of Data Steward, which I will label "Functional Data Steward", is locally aligned to a particular function or business area, with responsibility for their specific business area. For example, Marketing, HR or Operations. If a functionally-aligned data management structure has been implemented, then a Functional Data Owner (or possibly a Data Owner for a Functional Data Domain) may have been established, and Functional Data Stewards will work on behalf of this functional Data Owner. However, it is possible to have Functional Data Stewards that report into senior management at a local level, who assume functional data ownership responsibility without the need for a separate Data Owner role being formally established. The design of these kinds of roles can vary from organisation-to-organisation, tailored to the way that a particular business works.

The collaboration of people fulfilling these two different types of Data Stewardship roles enables the development of sensible, fit-for-purpose data rules; and also enables oversight and data management, including data quality management, at both a data domain-centric, cross-system level, as well as at a more local, function or business-aligned level. In the most effective Data Governance structures that I have seen, these two roles have been established in some shape or form, albeit not always using exactly the same labels as described here.

Wrapping up

So there you have it. A nice, simple overview of how data responsibilities work.

The foundations are really, very simple. The basic concepts align to how every organisation works and anyone should be able to understand them. The combination of these roles and responsibilities are important to make the whole work well; and by now I hope that you have a clear idea of how all the various data management roles fit together holistically.

However, there is still quite a lot of data jargon and theory in here, which only works if implemented sensibly and simply. You don't need to formalise every role that I've explained and in most cases it is more effective to formalise these responsibilities into roles that already exist and to use terminology that an organisation is already familiar with to land the concepts rather than trying to force a totally new way of thinking on people.

To bring this to a close, here are a few questions to ask yourself:

Do the descriptions in this article align to your understanding or have you had any "ah-hah" moments where you now have a clearer perspective on how these ideas fit together?

What will you do differently to simplify and clarify how data responsibilities work in your organisation?

Listen To Your Data Experts

Do you LISTEN to your "low-level" technical experts?

Often, when taking your first steps to address a large data management challenge, the best and fastest way to truly understand why things aren't working properly, or to identify the greatest opportunities to improve things, is to talk to people "at the coal face".

The low-level processors and developers and DBAs and ETL coders and data analysts.

The people who are "too in the weeds", who "don't know how to talk to the business", and who "don't 'get' the strategic big picture".

In my experience, they often have a much better idea about what really makes things work – or not work – than anyone else. More importantly, their ideas for what could be done to make things better are often far more practical than the grand plans that ivory tower architects or political senior managers can come up with.

Moreover, it's often these people who are depended on to "get the work done" anyway, no matter how they are perceived.

If you can take the time to listen, and to act as a translator; to turn their insights and ideas into strategies that link to the strategic drivers of your organisation, with sponsorship and support; and then execute on these ideas…

The results can be transformative.

Are you making the most of your technical experts'

views?

Data Management Is "Business As Usual Change"

"The Only Constant in Life Is Change."- Heraclitus

In many organisations, a clear split is made between "Business As Usual" (BAU) and "Change".

This is particularly true in Data Management, where it is now widely recognised that there is a need for permanent 'BAU' Data teams.

The trick is to avoid falling into the trap of allowing Data Management becoming a purely operational exercise.

A Data Management function needs to be a "BAU Change function".

It's BAU, in that the people working in the team are permanent members of staff, but it's Change in that its role is to continuously adapt to changes in the business and in the market, and to continuously drive value.

The minute Data Management becomes nothing more than an operational overhead, people will start forgetting why they are spending money on it and decrease investment.

It is true that some Data Management activities are operational (and these operational activities should be automated wherever possible), but having the mindset and approach of a Change function, which is constantly striving to deliver and demonstrate positive business value, is the path to sustained Data Management success.

How are you driving continuous improvement through

your Data Management efforts?

Part 5: Stakeholder Engagement

Why Stakeholder Management Is Crucial To Success

The most important thing to be successful in a large Data Management initiative is Stakeholder Management and Stakeholder Engagement.

The bigger and more complex and organisation, the more this is true.

Sure, subject matter expertise and technology are important too, but if you fail to manage your stakeholders effectively, no amount of subject matter expertise will help. You might be able to deliver a few local wins, and may even be able to realise some reasonable tangible benefits, but delivering the transformational value of data management, at scale, depends on people.

There will be key, influential and powerful people who either don't understand what you're doing, or don't agree with it, or think there are other things that are more important, or are just generally difficult to work with.

Data management is not something you can deliver in isolation. You need to be able to not only get on with people, but also to work with them in a productive way to overcome issues and get stuff done.

You will need senior support to prioritise your work. You will need budget and resources and technology. You will need people's co-operation and engagement to make things happen, and you will need to engage with people in a coordinated way to both ensure that the mix of people you are working with are aligned and to sustain this over time.

This is why the ability to engage with, collaborate with,

and positively and effectively influence and direct a range of people, at all levels, from senior execs down to junior developers, is crucial to the success of any large-scale data management initiative.

Do you agree?

What Is Stakeholder Management?

What is Stakeholder Management?

Despite its name, it's not actually about "managing" anyone.

It's about taking a structured and thoughtful approach to engaging with a set of people who are impacted by, and have some influence over, something you are trying to do, in order to influence their perceptions and actions in relation to whatever it is that you are trying to achieve.

For example, taking a structured approach to pro-actively engaging with people to obtain and sustain their support for your Data Transformation initiative, to maximise its chances of success.

There are various techniques for doing this, but here's a really simple one. To get you started, you could easily track this using a spreadsheet:

1. IDENTIFY and list out the people who are impacted by and/or will be influential in the delivery of whatever it is you are trying to achieve

2. "MAP" them (a column in your spreadsheet for each of the below) - for each person, determine:
- How impacted they are (High to Low)
- How influential they are (High to Low)
- How supportive they currently are (High to Low)
- Whether you need to change any of the above to help you achieve your outcomes

3. PLAN your actions: for each person, what will you do, including how and when will you engage with them and at what frequency, to either keep them where they are or

positively influence them (increase or decrease their impact, influence and/or level of support)

4. EXECUTE your planned actions!

5. REPEAT at a regular enough frequency to check whether your actions are working, to learn and adjust, both your list of target stakeholders and plans for each of them

You can do this formally or informally, depending on the scale of your project and how tricky your stakeholders are.

A few things to remember and watch out for:
- This is an approach to positively engage people, not to cynically manipulate anyone
- If you write your stakeholder map down, the information you capture will be sensitive so keep it confidential and treat it with care
- Remember that for some people, you may not need to do anything, or may want to reduce the impact of the work on them rather than needing to engage with them

So, as you can see, Stakeholder Management is really about managing the "process" of engaging with stakeholders, rather than managing the stakeholders themselves.

And the reality is, we all do this implicitly every day, whether we know it or not: this is just about taking a more structured and thoughtful approach.

How are you applying "Stakeholder Management" to the things you are trying to achieve?

Listen And Adjust To Succeed

PAY ATTENTION to what your stakeholders are saying – to their reactions and to the language they use.

STOP using Data Management buzzwords and jargon.

Every organisation is different. Every stakeholder is different. Everyone has their own, specific, set of personal and professional drivers.

If you want to 'obtain buy-in' and to effectively engage with the people who are key to the success of your Data Management initiative…

…first you must LISTEN and WATCH… and then you must TAILOR what you DO to directly meet their needs, using language that aligns to theirs.

How are you adapting your approach to meet the needs of your stakeholders and customers?

Getting It Right

"Can we make this quick please, I don't have much time."

We had 10mins booked. 20 minutes later, he called his secretary in and asked her to find us another 30 minutes later in the day to finish our conversation.

He thought I'd come to talk to him about Data Governance. It turned out I'd come to talk about what he was trying to do and how I could help him overcome some of the issues I knew his teams were facing.

This particular interaction was one I remember taking place around 2013 while I was working at Barclays. It was not the first, and it was far from the last.

Not all meetings with senior stakeholders have gone this well over the years- I had on many occasions before this made the mistake of trying to talk about the data stuff I was interested in, instead of making the discussion about them.

I've made mistakes since then too, and the nature of human interaction is such that I'm sure there will be many times that I don't quite hit the mark in the future too...

But one thing I will always try to do, is to prepare, to listen, and to do my best to really understand what the person I'm talking to is trying to do, so that I can engage with them about that, not about data management theory that they don't care about.

That doesn't mean completely avoiding talking about data, or pretending that data management isn't part of the solution- but it's about understanding the problem and providing tailored and relevant suggestions about addressing that problem, not trying to find a way to match a pre-defined solution to it.

What do you do, to engage with your senior stakeholders effectively?

Politics Are Inevitable

Are politics getting in the way of your ability to deliver your Data Strategy?

Competing priorities, 'difficult' stakeholders, conflicting actions, and a lack of focus from teams in other parts of the organisation who you are dependent on?

First, do you have senior enough sponsorship? Driving complex, large-scale change in any big organisation tends to need active top-down, executive-level sponsorship to establish the priority it needs and to ensure the people and other resources needed, are readily available to execute the work.

Second, are your senior stakeholders aligned? Data management often depends on collaboration across multiple teams, so if one member of ExCo is supportive but another is not, and there's a dependency between their teams, then you will still struggle to drive the change you need.

Third, are you using your senior sponsorship effectively to drive the work? This could involve a range of actions such as using their sponsorship to communicate the importance and urgency of the work to their teams, escalating to sponsors when there are blockers or issues to resolve (but be careful not to over-utilise this), regularly engaging sponsors to keep them informed of progress and to maintain an appropriate level of excitement and urgency to maintain their support, and more...

Politics exist in every organisation; some more so than others, but even in a company with a great culture, the fact is, when you get a large group of people working together, some level of politics will inevitably emerge and will need to be engaged with in order to get things delivered.

The question is: are you consciously "navigating the organisation" to deliver effectively? This can often make the difference between success and failure, especially when executing on a data strategy at enterprise scale, across multiple business units and functions.

What do you do, to avoid politics getting in the way of your ability to deliver?

Being Productively Unpopular

Are you willing to be a bit unpopular? Can you challenge people, whilst simultaneously building positive relationships with them?

If you are playing an effective Data Governance role, you've got to be ready to be unpopular with some people.

In fact, any oversight role – be it first line compliance, second line risk, internal audit or some other role – will most likely involve identifying and communicating problems, which some people won't like to hear about.

The trick is, that when you identify those really hard-hitting issues, which have a material impact on the business, you are able to raise them in a transparent way, whilst also receiving positive feedback from the stakeholders that they relate to, so you can play a constructive oversight and advisory role in working with them as they resolve the issues.

It's a balancing act, based on developing great relationships, based on respect and trust, where your stakeholders understand that you are always going to be fair in the way that you engage with them and in the way that you represent risks and issues with the various audiences who will be involved in both escalations and delivery.

Developing these relationships with stakeholders, starts well before any issues are identified, and if done properly, will continue long after you've finished working with them.

Long-term success is all about consistency. Are you always going to be fair and trustworthy? Will you always act with integrity and communicate issues in a way that prompts an appropriately urgent response, without creating undue panic and over-reaction?

With each new set of stakeholders, there will always be a period of getting to know each other, and there are going to be times that are easier than others… but investing time into building relationships in the right way, will always pay dividends in the long run.

Are you prepared to be unpopular, in order to do the right thing?

What do you do, to develop those stakeholder relationships, which will enable you to be successful in your role?

Part 6:
Data Governance

What Is Data Governance?

There are several Data Governance definitions out there, and they may be theoretically right, which is OK for Data professionals, but I've often found that non-data-experts tend to struggle to get their heads around what it is, based on those definitions.

Part of the challenge is, different people have different understandings of what "Governance" is, what "Data" is, and what the various Data-related activities (Data Management, Data Analytics etc); that there are, that might be brought under governance.

So, breaking this down simply:

I would say that Data Governance is all about:

(1) setting rules about Data, such as rules about how it should be captured, how it should be processed and how issues should be resolved;

(2) communicating those rules in a clear way, so the people who need to follow them, know that they need to;

(3) tracking whether or not the rules are being followed; and then,

(4) taking action if they are not being followed.

The rules could be set at a very low level, such as in a specific system or database; or very high level, such as rules about how every part of the organisation must log and manage Data Quality issues.

Data Governance can be implemented across one or several or all Data Management-related activities, depending on what you are trying to do.

So, you may govern the activities related to metadata, reference data, data architecture, data quality, the embedding of good data practices into change, data analytics, and so on.

This is part of the reason that people have struggled to define it succinctly in the past... but hopefully this explanation helps!

What Data Governance Is ABOUT

EFFECTIVE DATA GOVERNANCE IS *NOT* JUST ABOUT MEETINGS AND PAPERWORK...

...it's about driving timely and meaningful DECISIONS and ACTIONS...

...which CREATE CLARITY, RESOLVE PROBLEMS, ENABLE PROGRESS, REDUCE COSTS and DELIVER VALUE...

What are you doing to make sure your DATA GOVERNANCE initiative is EFFECTIVE?

A Near Miss

I remember the big glass doors and all the expectant, impatient faces.

Had I gone red in the face? I know I felt hot. I was forcing myself to breath slowly and calm myself down. This felt like a big moment.

It was the mid 'noughties' and I was already building a reputation as someone who could "do" Data Governance; but this meeting had not been as easy to prepare for as it should have been.

The months before this had all been great. The senior stakeholder engagement, the design of the Data Governance structures, the buy-in to what we were doing.

Even now, thinking back, I remember the PowerPoint slides I'd created to describe how everything was going to work, and they were textbook perfect. I guess you could say even better than that, because there weren't any textbooks on Data Governance back then!

This meeting had the "heads of" several key departments across the business – and they'd all turned up!

Just a few weeks earlier, when I'd started developing the agenda and content for the meeting with my team, we had realised there was a problem.

For all the brilliant org design and terms of references and everything, we realised that we hadn't implemented the metrics or remediation capability needed to make the meeting worthwhile.

These were some of the most senior people in the

business. Their time was precious, and they wouldn't appreciate sitting through an hour of waffle, with no action.

We had to act fast. In the weeks leading up to the meeting, we scrambled to gather facts that might provide insights the attendees hadn't seen before; to identify the root causes of issues they could make decisions on; and to formulate an agenda that would make them sit up and pay attention.

If this meeting went badly, we risked losing all the goodwill and support that we'd built up over the months leading up to it.

I don't remember the meeting itself. I just remember walking up to those big glass doors, printouts in hand, taking a breath and stepping in. Then I remember the feeling of elation as I left the room, knowing all the work had paid off.

More importantly, I remember thinking: I'm not going to make that mistake again!

And I haven't. I always make sure the capability to *deliver* is in place first, and that there is a real need to bring the people who are going to meet together. Otherwise, it's better not to meet at all.

One thing I have discovered though: if a meeting is really important, and is run really well, it often takes nearly the same level of planning and intensity it took to prepare for that nearly catastrophic meeting all those years ago.

The minute a Data Governance meeting becomes an administrative yawn-fest, with junior delegates and no meaningful decisions or actions, you know you're on the wrong track.

Have you had a similar experience?

What do you do, to make sure your Data Governance meetings are metrics-driven, focused and effective drivers of positive action?

Data Governance Committee Good Practice

Do you know what a good Governance committee looks like?

Notice that I'm deliberately not asking if you know what good *Data* Governance committee looks like...

Have you ever worked on a really well run transformation programme, with effective sponsorship and well run steering committees? What made the steering committees effective?

Have you ever participated in a corporate governance committees at a well run company? How were the committees run in a way that made them work well?

Or, have you worked on any particularly *badly run* programmes or for any *poorly governed* companies? What did you learn from them?

Data governance is just a type of governance. "Data" is the subject of focus, just as you might have a committee that focuses on Risks or Operations, but what makes it effective is the same - and if you don't know what good governance looks like, it's likely that you don't know what good data governance looks like.

Some things to consider:
- Do you have the right membership of your committee?
- Do you have a clear terms of reference, with well defined responsibilities?
- Do you have well formed agendas, which align to the purpose of the committee and the current risks and priorities that need to be addressed?
- Is high quality content and reliable metrics and data

being brought to your meetings, to enable effective decision making?
- Are your meetings well facilitated, driving decisions and actions?

Or, conversely:
- Are you spending a lot of time talking about theory and broad progress, but not making any decisions or taking any actions?
- Are the key decision-makers not turning up and sending delegates instead?
- Are actions being identified and logged, but not acted upon between meetings?

From a more subjective perspective, you'll generally know if your committees are working well, if people *want* to be there, and if people leave the meeting saying how great and productive it was. (Yes, committee meetings like this really do happen!)

Do you know what good governance looks like? If so, how are you applying it to your Data Governance efforts?

Governance Of Data WHAT?

There's no such thing as Data Governance!

"What?!!" - I hear you say... "Then what the **** were you doing when you were the Head of Data Governance?!"

What I mean is, Data Governance is not one thing. It's an umbrella term. It can cover a range of different things, depending on what you're trying to do.

Data Governance is, in fact: "The governance of... <insert one or more data management topics>"

For example, it could be the governance of metadata; or the governance of data architecture; or the governance of data quality; or all of these things, or several combinations of these things all at once, plus a few others.

This is why "Data Governance" is at the centre of the DAMA wheel.

But, depending on what your scope is, it might not cover every capability in the DAMA DMBOK... and it might cover some things that aren't covered by it, too... (other frameworks are available)...

Some people define the scope of Data Governance as covering the governance of ALL data management activities, and from a theoretical perspective, they may be right... but in practice, this is often not really the case; or it may be where you could aim for as a target state, but getting there will involve a series of steps.

Data Governance is also not just about the things that one or more data governance committee oversees - its scope can extend beyond this (and often does). Some Data Governance activities can be achieved without any committee. Some can be automated. Some are totally dependent on people and process. Some can be achieved through existing committees that don't focus on Data Governance...

So Data Governance, as a universally recognisable thing, really doesn't exist. It's an abstract concept, and a collection of practices, which only becomes real when it is implemented for a specific scope, to meet the needs of a specific organisation.

What are your thoughts on this?

A Better Way

How to deliver Enterprise Data Governance:

Old way:

- Paper-based policies & standards (Word/PDF)
- Manual questionnaires & control checks
- Decision by committee
- Success = Regulatory compliance

New way:

- Digital policies and controls, integrated into systems & processes
- Automated controls and evidence generated through actions
- Workflows and Individual Empowerment wherever possible
- Success = Tangible Business Outcomes
(with regulatory compliance as a happy by-product)

What are you doing to digitise, automate and empower data governance to deliver tangible business outcomes and benefits?

Change The Tone Of Your (Data) Governance Meetings

Governance meetings can be awful.

Dull, frustrating, a waste of time. Admin and checkbox-ticking. Creating audit trails for the sake of compliance.

Or they can be energising, problem-solving sessions. Valuable and necessary. The kinds of meetings that people don't want to miss, because they really matter.

What kind of governance meetings do you run?

Worst And Best Of Data Governance

The worst Data Governance initiatives are:

- Death by meetings
- Admin overload
- Checkbox-ticking
- Pedantic about semantics

I still see organisations falling into these traps even to this day.

If you're pouring time into Data Governance that doesn't deliver business value?

That sucks.

The key thing to realise is, maximising the value of your Data is dependent on effective Data Governance.

The word "EFFECTIVE" is key to note here, though.

INEFFECTIVE Data Governance can actually DAMAGE your attempts to deliver the outcomes of your Data initiative.

Nothing kills business buy-in faster than red tape, boring meetings and pointless paperwork.

You need a value-first approach:

- Clear business outcomes
- Prioritised and execution-focused
- Automated and minimal admin
- FUN because of how VALUE-FOCUSED and EFFECTIVE it is!

DATA VALUE SUCCESS v1.0

It all starts with clearly defined OUTCOMES, and there are some "good practice" steps that can be learnt, but it's a MINDSET of continuously coming back to the VALUE, that makes the real difference.

Hello, VALUE-FIRST Data Governance.

Goodbye, wasted time.

Effective Data Policy

A Data Policy, on its own, DOESN'T DO ANYTHING!

One question to consider: what's worse - having NO Data Policy, or having a Data Policy, with "mandatory requirements", that NO ONE IS FOLLOWING?!

Of course, having no policy at all won't look good to a regulator... but having policy requirements set out, which no-one is doing anything about, is also not a great place to be!

A Data Policy can be a powerful tool to set clear requirements and to establish governance at a large scale across an organisation... but the way the policy is designed and rolled out will be crucial to its success.

As with anything else in Data Management, you've got to start with a clear understanding of what you are trying to achieve first. What are the OUTCOMES you want to drive, and how will a policy help or hinder your achievement of those outcomes?

Then, once you are clear on the "why" and the outcomes, you need to think carefully about how a set of policy requirements will be rolled out, implemented and evidenced, in practice.

The culture and existing structures for policy rollout and enforcement in your organisation will make a big difference to how you do this.

You also need to consider the existing maturity of your organisation and the capacity of people to take on new requirements.

And are you designing your policy in a way that it could be automated, or are you going to be creating more admin and manual tasks in the way that you are writing it?

In principle, writing a Data Policy is a straightforward task. In practice, there's a lot of work involved in making it work.

Do you have a Data Policy in your organisation?

How have you designed it, and how are you rolling it out, to make sure it is successful and driving the right OUTCOMES?

Part 7:
Data Quality

Starting With Data Issues

A great place to start any Data initiative, is with DATA ISSUES.

NOTICE that I DID *NOT* say Data QUALITY issues there.

What do I mean by this?

A "Data Issue" is any BUSINESS PROBLEM, with a root cause that's RELATED to Data, in some way.

For example, you can't contact your Customers, because of missing Data. The Data Issue is that you can't contact your Customers. The root cause is RELATED to Data.

But the fact that Data is missing isn't the root cause. WHY is the Data missing? That's what you've got to get to the bottom to, and fix.

The root cause could be an issue with the technology, processes or people involved in the capture and processing of the Data. The Data itself isn't the issue.

But it *is* a Data-related issue. It's something where, if you fix the root cause problem that is resulting in missing Data (which IS a type of Data Quality issue), then you have fixed the Data Issue.

The great thing about Data Issues, as opposed to just Data Quality issues, is that you can identify them based on the PAIN that they are causing people in the business, and they are generally the things that are most important to people, because of this fact.

You don't need to go and setup Data Quality metrics to

FIND them, because people will already be complaining about them.

Which means you can get started NOW, without the need to establish lots of foundational capability first. Just go and ask people what's causing them the most pain!

It also means that, if you successfully fix a Data Issue, you will have resolved a real business problem, which people will benefit from and appreciate.

What are you doing to identify and resolve Data Issues?

What Is Data Issues Management?

Data Issue Management is about fixing the ROOT CAUSES of BUSINESS PROBLEMS related to Data.

Just to be clear, one missing piece of Data in one database table is not a Data Issue. That is an example of an occurrence of Data Quality issue.

A Data Issue is the underlying problem that is resulting in there being missing Data *every time* new Data is captured.

Or the problem that means Data that was captured correctly is corrupted 75% of the time, when it is processed across systems.

It should also be described in business terms.

For example, we are losing "X" amount of money every month because of… issue "Y".

Or we are getting "N" complaints every day, because of… issue "Z".

It's the loss of money, or the number of complaints, or wasted time, or other business outcome, that needs to be emphasised, before the Data part is highlighted.

This way, the focus can be on resolving something that really matters, not just a Data thing, where the impact of the Data thing isn't really understood.

So, Data Issues Management is about:
- Identifying Data Issues
- Performing root cause analysis on them
- Prioritising them

- Resolving the root causes, where the business case justifies it
- Celebrating the realisation of the benefits
- Repeating this process, as long as there is value in doing it

If you have a set of real, tangible Data Issues, which are actual business problems, that senior people care about; then you are going to get lots of people willing to invest money and resources and time into fixing them.

And then, as you successfully resolve them, you will deliver business benefit, and build credibility and support to do more.

You can implement Data Issues Management without any existing Data Management infrastructure.

You just have to go and talk to people to identify some real problems, add those problems onto a list, and get started.

And then, if you fix the root causes in the right way, you can start putting the Data Management foundations in place at the same time, and build your capability through the delivery of value, rather than needing a totally separate programme of work to do it.

Therein lies the value of Data Issues Management.

What can you do, to adjust your approach and make sure you are resolving the root causes of real Data Issues?

What Is Data Quality?

What is Data Quality?

At its most basic level, if your Data is complete and accurate, then it is good quality Data.

It's not quite as simple as that though.

For example, if your Data is complete and accurate, but has been captured in a format that can't be processed; or is delivered too late to be useful, then these factors may mean it's not as high a level of quality as it should be, for what it needs to be used for.

So "quality" is a measure of how fit-for-purpose your Data is, FOR A PARTICULAR USE CASE.

In some cases, having Data that is out-of-date isn't a problem. In others it is. If it's OK to get out-of-date Data, then its quality may be fine, for the given purpose; but if it's not OK, then it's not.

So Data Quality is totally linked to its context and what it's being used for. It's not an abstract thing.

Poor Data Quality can have a massive impact on you, your customers, your colleagues and your business.

For example, if you need to make a multi-million investment, the quality of your data could make all the difference between an amazingly positive return, and a terrible loss. If you have poor quality data, you could make a really bad decision, which loses you a lot of money.

Data quality is also often one of the causes of operational

issues, wasted time, and hidden costs related with needing to overcome gaps in information or "clean" data before it can be used. Even if the root cause of the data quality issues is not related to the data itself, there's no doubt that the impact of poor quality data can be operationally very painful.

It is also a common symptom of problems in processes and systems.

If a process or system is designed poorly, or if people using the process or system have not been trained properly, this is often where Data Quality issues arise.

In contrast, if a process and system is designed and working properly, you don't tend to get many Data Quality issues.

So Data Quality is important.

In fact, in some cases, it can be the whole point of a Data Management initiative.

Is Data Quality Management a core part of your Data initiative?

Effective Data Quality

Effective Data Quality Management is *NOT JUST ABOUT* creating lots of Data Quality metrics and tactically cleaning Data …

…it's about delivering BUSINESS VALUE by FIXING ROOT CAUSE ISSUES…

…which REDUCES WASTED TIME, INCREASES SPEED AND EFFECTIVENESS of DELIVERY, REDUCES ERRORS, REDUCES COMPLAINTS, REDUCES SECURITY BREACHES and MORE…

…good Data Quality underpins all effective business processes and customer interactions – so getting it right really does drive SIGNIFICANT VALUE…

Do you agree?

Is there anything you would add?

What are you doing to make sure your DATA QUALITY MANAGEMENT efforts are EFFECTIVE?

It's Not The Data's Fault!

Do you know the root cause of your Data issues?

One thing I can guarantee you: it's NOT THE DATA'S FAULT!

Whilst poor quality data can result in very severe negative impacts for a business, for customers or for other parties; when you investigate to find out what caused the data quality problems in the first place, they are never caused by poor quality data.

That's because data can't do anything alone. Data is just data - it can't perform any actions, unless a person, a process or a piece of software or other technology, does something with it. Once data is written into a data structure, it will just sit there until another operation is performed on it; and it didn't write itself into the data structure in the first place, so if it was written incorrectly, then whatever wrote it into the data structure is the cause, not the data itself.

So if you trace back, either a person input the data incorrectly, or they updated it in the wrong way; or a business process operated in a way that caused the data to be incorrect (and that business process will have been operated by people and/or technology); or a piece of technology, such as an automated update or data transfer, resulted in the data errors.

The cause of a data issue could be a simple, single point of failure in one of these places; or it could be the result of a complex web of inter-related people, process and technology issues, which need to be addressed together to ensure that the issues do not occur again.

This is why "data cleansing", if done on its own without addressing the root causes behind the data quality issues being "cleansed", is a futile and never-ending effort.

This is also why "data issues management" (notice that I didn't include the word "quality" in that sentence), is far broader than just getting some analysts to go into a database and "fix" the records that have been identified as being wrong.

The effective management and improvement of data issues involves root cause analysis and remediation of problems at source, whether they be people, process, or technology-related (and often they are a mix of all three).

Data Quality For Data Scientists

Data Quality for Data Scientists

As a Data Scientist, how much time do you spend on cleaning data?

Would you like to see LESS problems in the data you receive?

If so, here's an important question for you: when you find issues in the data, what do YOU do to feed back to the providers of that data, so that they can fix the problems at source? Or do you just clean the data without feeding back?

If you don't tell anyone, or don't do anything about the problems you find other than cleaning them for your own purposes, then had you considered that you may be part of the problem? If the problems aren't fixed at source, they're probably going to keep occurring, so every time you need to use that dataset, you're going to have to spend time cleaning up the same issues.

Even if it's just a polite communication to the data providers to let them know, at least that's a start. They might not even be aware!

Where data quality issues have been identified, the first crucial step to getting them resolved is COMMUNICATION of those data quality issues, back to wherever they came from.

Even if there are no formal data governance processes in place, this simple act can be the first step towards action being taken, which can result in transformational improvements.

Sometimes the root cause of millions of incorrect records could be something really small and simple to fix, such as a minor error in the logic of an ETL routine, which no-one noticed because no-one had ever complained about it.

Of course, sometimes issues are far more deep rooted and can be harder to fix; but how do you know, unless you say something about it?

Now that you have thought about this, are you going to do anything differently, next time you find issues in the data you've been provided with?

Targeted Data Quality Metrics

Stop wasting your time on obvious Data Quality metrics.

This is a very common mistake when following a "traditional" approach to developing Data Quality measures.

Two foundational Data Quality dimensions, which are often the starting point for Data Quality measurement, are "Completeness" and "Validity":

(1) "Completeness" (i.e. is the data that's supposed to be there, actually there? Or in other words, are there any mandatory fields where people haven't entered data when they should have); and

(2) "Validity" (or "Conformity" i.e. is the data valid, in other words, does the data that's been captured conform to the format that it should be captured in, for example is an email address a valid one, with things like an @ sign in the middle)

There is a lot of logic to starting here, because these are "quick wins" in many ways: easy to design measurement rules and to start measuring.

The trouble is, they can also be completely meaningless.

Where there is front-end validation that forces people to capture data in mandatory fields, and forces them to capture the data in a valid format, and does not allow them to submit the data until they have done so, these metrics will always "pass" these basic Data Quality tests.

So you could easily develop a whole slew of Completeness and Validity metrics, which are always going to "pass" and will create a sea of positive, "Green" results, because it is impossible for them to ever fail.

And where is the point of that?

The whole point of Data Quality Management is to identify real issues, so that they can be resolved, to deliver a positive business impact.

If you are just measuring things for the sake of measuring them, and never identifying anything wrong or delivering any improvements, you are totally wasting your time.

Don't get me wrong: where you are working in an environment where front-end validation is NOT in place, so there are various Completeness and Validity errors, these kinds of Data Quality measures are valuable and it does make sense to start here... but nowadays, nearly all professionally developed data capture forms have some level of validation built into them, so these metrics are not a great place to start.

Are you wasting your time on Data Quality metrics that don't deliver any real value?

Can you re-set, to develop measures that highlight real issues, so you can start driving some proper business benefits?

Fast-Track Your Data Quality Measure Designs

There is an often-overlooked way to quickly develop Data Quality measures that are meaningful and drive value.

It's NOT a theoretical approach or a technology solution.

It's simply this: go and talk to people who are USING the data and are experiencing problems with it.

Obvious, right? And yet, so many Data Quality projects seem to run without even talking to anyone who is impacted by Data Quality issues until after a set of metrics have been developed.

Follow the business problems, and you will find the Data Quality business rules and issues that will deliver the most value if they are resolved.

This will help you to de-prioritise the theoretical Data Quality metrics and to focus on the things that will highlight real issues.

BUT - *don't* just depend on people's opinions.

It's also important that you take people's views and rapidly create some DQ measures on real data, and share the results with them, so that you can gather feedback and iterate and improve the metrics.

Often, it's when you apply a set of business rules to real data and generate real results, that the business can look at those results and identify the real problems and refine the rules to make them "fit".

The key though: do talk to people. Understand what really

matters; and act on that, not just on Data Quality theory.

Are you running a Data Quality project at the moment?

If so, are you engaging with the people who are impacted by the Data Quality issues, to make sure the work you are doing is actually going to help?

USE Your Data Quality Tool!

Why aren't you USING your Data Quality tool?

Could you deliver value 10x faster, by making proper use of Data Quality profiling?

Two common approaches, which DO make logical sense, but can be SLOW, and could also result in missed opportunities:

(1) Go and talk to business users to understand their Data Quality business rules, before you do anything with the Data itself

(2) Focus on "Critical Data Elements" (CDEs) or "Key Data Elements" (KDEs), and ONLY seek to measure them – and nothing else!

But what about the power of the Data Quality tool that you have invested in?

Most DQ tools have the ability to run a quick data quality profile over a dataset, automatically identifying patterns, missing values and potential data quality issues.

(1) You can create a data quality profile like this and take it to the business, to start the discussions with them, based on real data, not just starting with a blank sheet of paper.

(2) This will give you insight on ALL of the data in a dataset, "for free". Restricting your profile to only CDEs is actually *HARDER* than using the out-of-the-box capability over ALL of the data!

Of course, a Data Quality tool is not a silver bullet, and

does not replace the need to talk to people who are impacted by Data Quality issues. This dialogue is totally essential and is the only way to get to a set of DQ measures that are meaningful and drive value; but using a DQ tool properly can radically accelerate efforts and can enable you to be far more effective than if you don't use a tool like this.

Do you have a Data Quality tool that you can make use of?

If so, are you making the best use of it, to accelerate your efforts and drive more value, faster?

Part 8: Data Architecture

What Is Data Architecture?

The more complex a Data solution, the more important Data Architecture becomes.

But what is Data Architecture, exactly?

The analogy of building something physical is a good place to start.

Before you build a physical structure, you need to design it, and you would be wise to get an Architect to do this.

To design a structure well, you need to understand what the building will be used for, and create a design, which satisfies those needs, within the constraints of the building project, making the best use of the materials and building techniques available.

You may need to lay new foundations, or may have existing foundations to build on. You may have some level of choice about the building materials you can use, and may have some materials and building techniques that you don't have any choice but to use.
The key task of an Architect is to work out how the building will be laid out and how the various building materials will be brought together to deliver the outcome you need.

A poorly designed Architecture could result in a building that doesn't fit together; that doesn't meet the needs of its users; or worse, that is dangerous and could fall down!

Without an Architecture, builders could have a go at building something, but it's far less likely to meet the needs of whoever is going to use it; and it's far more likely that problems will be encountered along the way, which could result in delays and unexpected costs and issues.

Also, as building progresses, problems may arise, requiring an Architect to update the Architecture to ensure the building will still be fit-for-purpose.

Data Architecture exists to do the same thing, for Data.

A Data Architecture defines what data is captured; where and how; how it will be structured and modelled; how it will flow across the various technologies and processes that are used; and what tools will be used to manage it effectively.

Data may need to be structured in different ways for different types of processing; and Data may need to be transformed, combined and analysed.

There may be things that are done to the Data that could result in Data Integrity and Data Quality issues, so a well formed Data Architecture will include mechanisms for avoiding these issues, or for identifying and resolving them if they do occur.

When designing solutions that cut across multiple systems (or that integrates Data from multiple sources), "Data Architecture" can blur into the domains of Infrastructure Architecture, Application Architecture, Integration Architecture, and even Process Architecture... because the specific technologies that are used and the ways these technologies come together, are important factors in making sure Data is collected and processed in the most effective way.

However, regardless of the how the discipline is categorised, the whole point is: the design of Data solutions, which deliver good outcomes.

If you're achieving this, then you've probably got a good

DATA VALUE SUCCESS v1.0

Data Architecture.

… DATA VALUE SUCCESS v1.0

Understanding The Real Role Of Data Architecture

"The map is not the territory." - Alfred Korzybski

"All models are wrong, but some are useful." - George E. P. Box

I love these two quotations.

Data architecture diagrams, data models, analogies, fables, statistical models, process models...

...we often use models, diagrams, stories, allegories, pictures, and other constructs to make sense of the world; to understand problems and make decisions; to govern and manage and direct and track...

However, it's important for us to understand both the value and the limitations of the techniques that we use; and to avoid the trap of either taking things too literally or jumping to the wrong conclusion due to mis-interpretations.

A classic (and often quoted) example where a statistical model can be used to reach the wrong conclusions, is where "correlation" is mistaken for "causation".

BUT models are also NOT ONLY extremely powerful, when used correctly, but ESSENTIAL for us as human beings. We each have our own mental model, which is our way of perceiving things, and is used to help us make decisions and interact with the world, developed based on all of our experiences and based on our own learning preferences.

Think about the models you use every day.

Are there any that are unhelpful or driving the wrong outcomes?

Are there any that could be used more effectively?

Or are there things where you think a new model could help?

People – Process – Technology – DATA

People - Process - Technology - Data

I was first introduced to this simple yet effective framework over 18 years ago when I first started in consulting.

If you are either diagnosing the cause of a problem, or designing a solution for something, thinking about what needs to be considered across each of these topics is a great way to make sure you haven't missed something important.

There are various more sophisticated approaches for impact analysis and design, but you can't go far wrong if you have considered at least these 4 things.

Every problem you can think will be caused by something that's gone wrong or is missing about at least one of these things... and every solution to a problem should at least consider these things in some shape or form (even if you don't need to address all of them, it's a good discipline to think about them).

Do you use the categories of People / Process / Technology / Data, when you are analysing problems or developing solutions?

How useful do you find it, or is there a better approach you tend to use?

The Cost Of Legacy Technology

Why does maintaining legacy technology cost so much?

Let's compare it to a building.

Imagine you have an old converted barn, which has a thatched roof.

In the past, thatching was one of the most advanced techniques for roofing, providing outstanding insulation and protection from the elements. Thatching was also a common skill, so maintaining a roof built using this technique was relatively cheap.

Nowadays, a thatched roof is no longer cutting edge. More modern methods last longer with less need for maintenance. The skills needed to maintain a thatched roof are scarce, so expert craftsmen can charge more.

Also, if you ever wanted to extend your house, to add more space or use it for other purposes, connecting it to modern roofing structures will be hard and expensive, and will make it even harder and more costly to maintain in the future.

Unlike a thatched roof, your legacy technology doesn't 'look nice', so other than the fact that it 'still works', the benefits of continuing to invest in it may not outweigh the costs of replacing it with more modern technology that is faster, cheaper and easier to maintain now and in the future.

Does this analogy work for you? What do you think?

DATA VALUE SUCCESS v1.0

The Data Tells The Real Story!

LOOK at your ACTUAL DATA to understand how your business is operating.

Architecture diagrams and process maps and high-level reports all provide interesting and partially useful views of how data is being captured, managed and used...

BUT it's only by looking at the DATA itself, as it actually exists in physical tables and systems and feeds, that you can see what's really happening.

Your data is a reflection of how your business operates. It is a lens into what's actually going on, and enables you to step out of theory and into reality.

Are you stuck in theory land, developing ivory tower PowerPoint decks and Visio diagrams that conceptually describe what's going on, or are you really engaging with your Data to uncover the actionable truth?

Master And Reference Data

Master and Reference Data are your MOST IMPORTANT Data.

And the bigger your business, the more important Master and Reference Data are.

If you want to do any kind of analysis, you will find that, the better your Master and Reference Data are, the easier it will be to analyse all of your Data, to find patterns and insights.

For example, let's take a "transaction", which at its most basic level is just a record of a number moving from one account to another, for example one account making a payment and another receiving it.

If the receiving Account number is wrong, the wrong party could get paid. Plus, if you don't tag your transaction with information about WHERE it took place (location data), or WHO was involved in the transaction, or any other key bits of information that you might want to know about it... then all you will know is that some numbers moved from one account to another.

Which can be a problem, if you want to use your Data to actually run your business effectively.

Inaccurate Master and Reference Data is often the cause of operational issues, poor customer experience, and is a common cause of errors in management reports.

From an operational standpoint, if you've got the wrong address for a customer, you could send a product to the wrong place.

Or, from a reporting standpoint, the same error, if occurring at scale, could make one geography look more profitable than another, when rolled up into a companywide report.

Do you value your Master and Reference Data?

What do you do, to make sure it's managed properly?

Mastering Data

If I were being pedantic, I would say that "Master Data" isn't a "type" of Data, because *any* Data could potentially be Master Data.

"Mastering", is a thing you *do* to Data, in order to establish which version of the Data is the most reliable version, and to make sure that is the version that everyone uses.

Which is why people can sometimes get confused when talking about "Reference Data"... surely that's Master Data, too?

Well, yes, it could be, if you've "Mastered" it; but if you haven't "Mastered" it, it might not be...

There are several ways that you can "Master" Data, but the one that tends to be the easiest for people to understand – and the one that gives it its name – is where you create a single, central version of the Data, which is know as the "Master" version; and then you make sure all other places where the Data appears, aligns to the "Master" version.

So when you hear terms like "Golden Source of truth" and "Authoritative Source", and "System of Record", it's referring to the idea of having a version of the Data, which is the recognised version that everyone must use.

So, theoretically, if you have lots of copies of the same transaction appearing across multiple systems, then decide that the copy in one system is the "Master" version, then even Transactional Data could be Master Data!

However, the classic way of dividing up different high level "types" of data is to separate out: Transaction Data, Reference Data, Master Data and Meta Data.

This is because there are sets of data, which have common properties, which means that the way that you manage them is different.

So there are several datasets, which are commonly considered to the "Master Data" (despite what I've just said!)

These tend to be key business concepts, which describe the parties, relationships and agreements that organisations get involved in.

For example, types of parties could include: Customers, Employees, Suppliers, Businesses, Legal Entities, and so on.

These Master Data entities, tend to be more complex than other types of Data, because you need to capture lots of bits of information about them.

In contrast, the easiest way to think of Reference Data, is the codes and values that are either used to "look up" something else, or the things that appear in a drop-down list.

So, for example, a list of Countries, is a Reference dataset, which could be used in multiple places, for multiple purposes – but it is just a list, maybe with a description and a mapping to some other codes and lists – it does not represent a complex concept like a Customer.

DATA VALUE SUCCESS v1.0

Why Standardise?

When it comes to Data, standardisation is everything.

No matter how diverse your data sources and datasets, when you come to integrate them, to do any kind of analysis, you need a way to match and compare across them, and this invariably means you will need to apply some kind of structure to enable you to do anything meaningful across them.

Yes, there are techniques to infer relationships across datasets, but the less standardisation you have, the less accurate these techniques will be; and in some cases, a lack of standardisation will mean some data simply will not be captured, making some types of analysis impossible (for example, where the level of granularity or detail a dataset goes down to hasn't been specified and you want to perform analysis at a level of detail that hasn't been captured).

If standards have already been applied, for example if transactions have been categorised against standard reference data before they need to be integrated, you will save a MASSIVE amount of time and effort, whilst SIGNIFICANTLY reducing the chance of data quality issues.

This a side of data management which may seem a bit "dull" to the uninitiated, but the value of doing it is significant and grows as the scale and complexity of the data you are dealing with grows.

Or rather, the cost of *not* doing it, can be huge and compounds with the greater number (Volume) and diversity (Variety) of data that you need to bring together...

Anyone that has been involved in efforts to retrospectively resolve the problem of a *lack* of standardisation will know just how painful and costly it is to sort out if it's been allowed to go on for too long.

Standardisation needs to be designed and enforced. It's often not easy to do at scale, but the pain of doing it is far less than the pain of not doing it.

Have you experienced the pain caused by a lack of standardisation when trying to perform reporting or analysis across multiple datasets?

What are you doing to avoid these kinds of problems?

How To Make Your Data Lineage Valuable

Are you wasting time and money on your data lineage?

Asking the right questions can help you focus your efforts in the right way:

Are you trying to minimise the number of manual steps in your data flows? Are you capturing your lineage in a way that helps with this?

Are you trying to make sure you have the right controls across your data architecture, such as data quality, data integrity and reconciliation controls? Does your data lineage capture these so you can see where they are and where they might be missing?

Are you taking steps to make sure key processes and reports are using data from the right sources? Does your data lineage give you insight into which data sources are the points of initial data capture or nominated authoritative sources?

Are you trying to improve your ability to perform impact analysis, to enable faster and more effective delivery of change, or to better respond to incidents?

Or are you capturing data lineage just because it's a regulatory requirement?

It's important to be clear about your reason for investing in data lineage and be intentional about how you capture, maintain and use it, to deliver the outcomes that you're aiming for.

Scheduling The Value Of Data Lineage

Do you SCHEDULE the VALUE?

I was thinking of Data Lineage when I came to this post, but the principle applies to anything you are doing.

When you are investing any time, money, or other resources, into any activity... how do you make sure it delivers value, in a reasonable timeframe?

There are many activities in the Data Management space, which can be very time- and effort-intensive. They are about building the foundations; establishing the groundwork; setting things up for success; and all those other strategic planning buzzwords.

The trouble is, you can invest in foundations forever, but if you don't build anything of value of them, then you're not actually gaining anything. You are wasting your investment. It's all just a cost, and not delivering value.

A simple test with anything like this, is: can you schedule the delivery of value?

Even if you are building foundations for something, you are building the foundations FOR SOMETHING, right?

What is that something? Taking Data Lineage as an example, are you going to remove manual data flows, or remove duplicate data sources, or identify the optimal place to implement some data quality controls, or something else?

If so, when will you actually do some of those things? Can you do it this week, this month, this quarter?

If you can't commit to delivering value in a reasonable timescale, is your investment really worth it? Or is there a way you could do the work differently to deliver value?

I would strongly encourage you to think about this, on a regular basis. At a minimum, once a month, review what you are doing, and ask the question: WHEN will this deliver tangible value?

If you don't have an answer, then update your plans so that you DO have an answer, and see just how much more effective you become.

DATA VALUE SUCCESS v1.0

Metadata Wisdom

"Data without metadata is like a box of chocolates, you never know what you're gonna get!"

- Forrest Gump (if he'd been a Data Professional)

Part 9:
Data Insights & Reporting

Keep The Outcome In Mind

So you've BUILT A DASHBOARD...

... SO WHAT?

... What DECISIONS or ACTIONS have been taken as a result?

...How much MONEY has been SAVED or GENERATED?...

...Who is actually USING it?

...Who has BENEFITED from it?

Always ask the "SO WHAT?" questions... not matter what you're doing...

DATA VALUE SUCCESS v1.0

Beware Data Misuse

BEWARE THE MISUSE OF DATA TO MAKE A POINT!

1. Did you know that 88.2% of statistics are made up?*

2. Using data to back up an argument can increase its perceived validity by up to 78.4%.

3. Even more alarming, 66.6% of these 3 statements are verifiably false, because 100% of the above 2 statements were made up!

(* The first one of these originally came from the UK comedian Vic Reeves).

Before you react to this with your logical mind, think for a moment about how the statements above made you FEEL when you first read them.

As human beings, we can't help but initially react differently to statements backed up with numbers, even if it turns out the numbers are wrong.

The use of data is a powerful tool for driving decisions.

Used responsibly and properly, data analysis can provide genuine insights, which can materially improve understanding, decision making and action.

However, data can also be mis-used.

If you are using data to back up a point, take the time to ensure you are performing your analysis objectively, and either present the facts based on a proper statistical analysis, and/or provide clear explanations about the potential shortcomings in the analysis. This is where both a bit of an understanding of statistics, and more importantly taking a professional and ethical approach to analytics, become important.

If you are a consumer of some analysis, make sure you don't take everything you are presented at face value. Review the data, challenge the methodology and assumptions, and be really thoughtful about what you do with the insights- especially for those decisions that could have a really big impact.

—

Did you know that 100% of the people I asked about this post agreed with it?

That is the absolute truth. Just don't ask me how many people I asked!

Why Less Is Often More

With Data Visualisation, LESS is often MORE. Expanding on this:

When you have a lot of data and a load of potential insights to share, the temptation may be to try to present all of those data and insights together.

This can lead to very busy charts and graphs and other visualisations... combinations of multiple chart types on one page... multiple dimensions... loads of colours and gradients... overlays, animated builds, and more...

...but the human brain just isn't that great at dealing with all these layers of visuals.

For example, people generally deal very well with 2 dimensions.

X and Y. Up and across.

It's because it's really easy to process.

Can people deal with more?

Yes, of course.

BUT

Often, it's better to create more than one visualisation, each with less on it, rather than trying to load everything into a single, complex visual.

Think: instead of trying to visualise 4 dimensions at once, what about several 2-dimensional visualisations of these variables, on different pages or tabs?

You can present these multiple separate visualisations in an order, to build up a story.

You can make them available to compare and contrast, to analyse alongside each other.

If you really get more from combining these various variables, maybe present the 2-dimensional visualisations first, then build up to more complex multi-dimensional visualisations, by layering them, to allow people to get used to the simpler models first?

I'm not saying that complex multi-dimensional visualisations is always wrong - in fact, it is sometimes necessary - I'm just saying that it often pays to simplify.

And in my experience, especially when presenting information to a less data literate audience, less is almost always easier to interpret and understand.

Creative Data Analysis

Data Analysis is a CREATIVE, BUSINESS-FOCUSSED activity.

What? but surely it's a technical thing?

Well, it absolutely does require some technical skills.

And the more complex the analytics, and the more advanced the analytical models you are using, the more technical skills you need.

HOWEVER:

1. If you are not clear on the BUSINESS PROBLEM you are trying to solve, or the BUSINESS INSIGHT or BUSINESS OUTCOME you are aiming for - then you are probably wasting your time!

2. There are always many ways to analyse your data - so you will often need to EXPLORE it, EXPERIMENT and PLAY with it, in order to derive insights that are useful.

The creative part of this becomes even more important when you are dealing with diverse data, and when you are experimenting with the use of different analytical models and approaches.

What happens when you get unexpected results?

What happens when an approach doesn't work, or works better than expected?

What happens when you combine the Data in different ways, and slice and dice it differently?

Whilst there are very useful methodologies for data analysis out there, they are just frameworks to help structure the work.

The reality is, data analytics is rarely a linear, paint-by-numbers process. Which is why creativity plays such an important part.

Can you think of a case, where data analytics doesn't require any creativity at all?

DATA VALUE SUCCESS v1.0

This May Work Better As A Social Media Post

I bet you £492755392652473 that you didn't read that number. You just skipped right over it. You didn't even realise I put a letter in it. No, I didn't, but you went back and looked.

When you are presenting data to someone, you need to bear this is mind.

As human beings, we are great at skimming information and rapidly jumping to conclusions.

So if you present data to someone in the same way as the first paragraph here, if the number is somehow important for the point you're making, then this is not a great way to do it.

The way you present your facts is crucial. For example, is a number's size relative to something else important? Would a visualisation help? Or is the number itself not really important other than to substantiate some other point you're making, in which case maybe it's OK for people to skim it, as long as it's accurate if they ever want to go back and check it?

What do you do, to make sure you present data in a way that achieves the right impact with your audience?

#data #presentation #effectiveness #trick

Note: I'm not sure where the first paragraph originally came from- I saw a similar meme and tried to track its source but there are a load of variations of it across the Internet (so now here's another one!)

Use The Right Type Of Visualisation

Um, I don't think a pie chart is the best way of visualising that trend data that you've got there.

How many times have you seen data presented in a chart or graph that makes absolutely no sense at all?

Using the right types of visualisations can transform the way we interpret data. It can help uncover insights and enable new levels of understanding.

But using the wrong types of visualisations can be confusing, pointless, or at worst, downright misleading. In these cases, you may be better off just sharing the data as a simple table for people to interpret themselves, rather than using a poor choice of visual representation.

What are some of the worst examples of data visualisation that you've seen?

DATA VALUE SUCCESS v1.0

You Need Quality Data For Quality Insights

DATA SCIENCE can be a SILVER BULLET for some problems.

Poor Data Quality SWAPS THE SILVER FOR JELLY and the GUN for A BOW, but doesn't let anyone know until they try to SHOOT IT!

Have you ever had a Data Science project miss the mark due to poor Data Quality?

Part 10:
Data Literacy & Culture

Data Culture

A Data Culture is just a part of a company's overall Culture.

And a company's Culture is shaped by what people *DO*.

Look at people's actual behaviour, and you'll see a company's real culture.

Listen to what they say, and you'll hear it.

This is why, if you want to change the (Data) Culture of an organisation, doing the tick-box stuff is never enough.

You can publish some values, and run some training, and tell everyone how important a Data Culture is...

...but what you really need, is for people to start DOING things differently.

This is where you need role modelling. You need some specifically different actions, which can be done visibly, and to create new habits around the new behaviours.

And behaviour change can be hard, even when the new behaviour isn't really that hard. It's new and different and (gasp) a change.

All of the comms and training and stuff to foster a particular Culture is still important...

...but without role modelling and targeted behavioural change, you're just wasting your time.

It's when people start saying thins like: "that's how we do things here", that you know you're onto something.

When you hear people telling stories about what people have done, which really do demonstrate the behaviours you want, and where the stories you hear aren't all complaints about the things that are wrong with the Data and the Systems, they're about the innovative ways that they've been used for good.

A Data Culture rarely happens by accident, but it invariably starts with a small number of people showing other people a better way, and with the senior support to keep doing it.

Are you trying to deliver a Data Culture?

What are you doing to avoid falling into the trap of superficial actions?

What Is Data Literacy?

Imagine these two scenarios:

First: a CEO who receives a set of Data, to use to make a decision, which could result in multiple millions of extra revenue, or multiple millions in losses, depending on the decision they make.

Second: a contact centre agent who receives a complaint from a customer and needs to use the Data they provided, along with Data in the company, to work out what happened and to see if they can resolve the complaint.

In each case, the ability to use the Data effectively is crucial to success; and if the Data is not used properly, it could result in significant negative outcomes.

And it's not just about using the Data.

It's about analysing the Data and challenging it. It's about identifying opportunities to bring it together with other Data, to derive further insights and opportunities.

For example, a really basic error that I've seen many times, is where a report is presented, but numbers in different tables on the page don't add up.

This is such a basic thing, but if the numbers don't add up, you can't rely on whatever the report is telling you.

Another case is where there are several parts of a report, which are related. Understanding those relationships and taking them into account when analysing Data is another simple thing, which can have a massive impact on the effective use of a report.

Let's take an easy example of this: if the cost of a product goes up, and the quantity of the product being sold does not go down, then revenue should go up. If it doesn't, then either the Data is wrong, or there is some other factor that you need to investigate and understand.

As with any type of Literacy, there are different levels of Data Literacy, from foundational through to advanced. If you don't do much with Data, then it may not matter too much if you aren't very Data literate. If you are a Data Scientist, then having an advanced level of Data Literacy is pretty important!

Going back to the first two examples, you can see that higher levels of Data Literacy can lead to better business decisions, better operations and better customer service.

It's also a great thing for you and every individual at a personal level: the more Data Literate you are, the more effective you can be, leading to personal as well as collective success.

What are you doing to improve your own Data Literacy?

And what are you doing to encourage Data Literacy in your organisation?

Context Is Everything

It doesn't matter how much knowledge and experience you have.

It doesn't matter if you think the solution to a problem is "obvious" based on prior experience.

You need others on your side, if you want to get anywhere.

You need to invest the time and effort into both properly understanding the specific context within which you are working, and into explaining the options and solutions to the people you need support and participation from.

What are you doing to avoid the trap of thinking something that's "obvious" to you, is obvious to everyone else?

Are you doing anything to build support through engagement and collaboration?

Just Complex Enough

"Everything should be made as simple as possible, but not simpler." - Albert Einstein

This is just as true for Data Management as anything else.
It's important to work out ways to simply communicate concepts, so that people can understand them and act upon them.

But the reality is, the nature of Data often means that you can't avoid a level of complexity, which needs to be acknowledged and dealt with.

A key trick is to expose sufficient complexity to a given audience, for them to understand enough that they can make decisions and act appropriately, whilst avoiding overwhelming them with too much detail.

If things are too complicated, you will lose people; but if you dumb things down too much, you could create the wrong perceptions about the work and could ultimately drive the wrong decisions or actions.

Have you encountered this challenge before?

What have you done to strike the right balance?

Making e-Learning Work

Who enjoys completing mandatory e-learning modules about Data?

Data management training, data privacy training, data security training, data BOREDOM.

I'm a Data professional, and in the past I've built training modules on these kinds of topics, and even so, I can tell you that I haven't enjoyed most of the modules I've had to complete in recent years!

So how can they possibly be effective, if people hate doing them?!

The reality is, in many organisations, there are so many mandatory training modules, most people just try to click through them as quickly as possible, to get them over with.

Don't get me wrong- I do think mandatory training has its place.

It is one way to ensure that everyone across a company has received some minimum level of awareness about key points that they really need to know.

But on its own, it's clearly not enough.

And if it is one of the only mechanisms available to you, it makes it even more important for you to think carefully about how you use it, to maximise its value and effectiveness.

THINK:

- SHORT- can you keep it to under 5mins? (People will thank you and will remember how painless it was in comparison with other courses. Drop the slow animations and transitions too!)

- PUNCHY- what are the key points people REALLY need to know? Don't cover more than is needed!

- DIFFERENT- how do you make it stand out from all the other vanilla training modules?

- FUN and/or SHOCKING- can you make it gripping?

- ACTION- what specifically do you want people to DO as a result of the training?

- EXAMPLES- a really relevant story will always stick in people's minds better than just dry theory

- REPEATED- create messages and images that will stick in people's minds and repeat them, both in the training itself, and in follow up comms and collateral and things

- INTERACTIVE- I put this last, because although it is a good way to engage people and help ideas stick, it also lengthens the training course time and can annoy people if they want to get through the course quickly. This is where other follow-up interventions can come in.

Do you have mandatory Data training modules?

How are you making sure they are effective and not just another irritating mandatory admin task for people to complete?

Any other opinions or ideas?

How Do You Drive Real Cultural Change?

With Data Culture, the easy and obvious things, on their own, don't work.

What do I mean by easy and obvious?

Having an intranet site. Sending out comms. Running an event. Running some training.

All important components of a Culture Change initiative, but not enough on their own.

On their own, these things tick the box of having "done something", but don't actually CHANGE anything.

So what can you do, to really move the needle?

You can do the following.

NOTE: each of these things sound simple, but doing them properly requires genuine effort, commitment and long-term follow-through.

1. Senior Role Modelling

By this I mean really visible, vocal sponsorship by senior leaders; complemented by actions that a congruent to the messages.

Senior leaders not only advocating the behaviours that are expected, but also leading through their actions.

People follow the example set by their leaders.

2. Repeat, Repeat, Repeat

People don't remember something the first time they hear it or see it – so only telling people something once, won't make the message stick.

It's important that whatever messages you want to get out there are repeated, through multiple channels and media.

The same key points. The same logos and images.

The more you repeat, the more it will stick.

3. Familiarity Isn't Threatening

People don't like change. It's in our nature as humans to be comfortable with the familiar.

So, whilst it is important to be able to grab people's attention, linking to things people are familiar with, and using channels that are "the norm", will improve engagement.

4. Couple Culture Change with REAL Change

If all you are doing is telling people to behave differently, what does that actually mean?

Often, REAL change happens, when REAL change happens, like when people have to start following a new process, or use a new system. There is no choice but to work differently.

Deliver changes to systems or processes, to deliver change to culture.

5. Tie Behaviours To Performance

In simple terms, I'm talking about making Data Culture part of people's performance objectives. If people's bonuses and pay rises – or lack thereof – are linked to a set of Data Culture behaviours or outcomes, it will drive a chance in behaviour.

You do need to be careful with this one, to make sure it's done in a positive way and doesn't drive the *wrong* kinds of behaviour change, but done properly, this is a really effective.

6. Measure and improve

This one comes with a two big caveats: (1) it's important you choose and design the right measures (2) you need to actually look at and USE the measures, for them to be helpful.

But there's no doubt that measuring the impact of your efforts is important: if you don't measure what you're doing, how will you know whether you are being effective or not?

Are you trying to drive a Data Culture?

How many of these things are you doing, or not doing?

What will you do differently now?

Part 11: Working In Data Management

If Data Management Is So Easy, Why Is It So Hard?

Why is Enterprise-wide Data Management so HARD?

Especially when many of the "things" you need to do are so EASY (conceptually, at least)?

There are many reasons, but here are three for starters:

1. It involves getting a LARGE NUMBER OF PEOPLE to COOPERATE. When lots of people are involved, with different perspectives and agendas, getting people to align and collaborate is challenging – and this is why stakeholder engagement is so important to be successful.

2. It requires DISCIPLINE and PERSISTENCE. As human beings, we're not generally great at these things. This is why creating a path of least resistance, and making it as easy as possible for people to "do the right thing", will massively increase your chances of success. We need to work with human nature, not against it.

3. Addressing data management ENTERPRISE-WIDE is BIG. It's easy to become overwhelmed by the task, or to over-invest in the wrong priorities; to pour effort in and become discouraged by the lack of progress. This is why it's important to break the problem down, to ensure tangible and visible value is delivered early and often, and why there's such a strong trend towards agile approaches. When attempts to "eat the elephant whole", or "boil the ocean", have repeatedly failed, a different approach is needed.

The thing is, when you get a glimpse of data management working, the results are astounding. The hype isn't really hype at all, it's just that not many organisations have been able to live up to it. And here is the challenge: the bigger you go, the greater the payoff; but the harder it is to deliver.

The "things" you need to do are easy on paper. You can read them in a textbook. But doing them depends on leadership and influence at scale; it depends on discipline and persistence; and it takes experience to apply the conceptually easy things that you can find in a textbook, in the real world.

What are you doing to address these challenges?

Getting Through To Sceptics

The best thing about working in Data Management is seeing people's reactions when it really starts paying off.

Those lightbulb moments when even the sceptics can't help themselves but say: "Wow, this is actually pretty awesome, isn't it?!"

Especially when the benefits were delivered far faster and easier than expected, or have turned out to be dramatically bigger than people thought they would be.

Even better when previous attempts to deliver value through data have failed, and people were losing faith... that moment of realisation that the potential IS still there; it IS possible; and all the effort and investment WAS worth it, after all...

It's a great feeling.

Work Smart

"GETTING STUFF DONE" does not always equal success.

Delivery of VALUABLE OUTCOMES = SUCCESS.

Work smarter, not harder.

Being BUSY is NOT the same as being EFFECTIVE.

This is just as true in Data Management & Analytics as it is in any other part of your life...

...and yet, I still see so much data management "busy work". My advice: stop the busy work, focus on the smart work.

PRIORITISE and *then* act, if you want to succeed.

There Are No Dumb Questions

Have confidence asking the dumb questions.

It's the smart thing to do!

You will look a lot sillier if you don't ask those questions and it turns out you've been pretending to understand something that you don't.

Don't try too hard to project an image of 'knowing'. Take your time to actually understand.

If you think you understand something, try asking clarification questions and restating your understanding in different words to confirm that you've got it right. This will come across as far more 'knowing' than jumping to conclusions without validating your assumptions.

Even experts don't know all the answers when they approach a new problem. Part of their expertise will be realised through asking the right questions and methodically exploring options.

How do you feel about asking the so-called "dumb" questions?

Regulatory Requirements Can Drive Value

Do you have a heap of regulatory commitments that you need to meet relating to data management?

Are you clear on WHY your regulator expects you to do those things?

Is your current approach delivering any real value?

If you're investing money and resources into data management activities that aren't delivering any benefit other than ticking some regulatory boxes, it may be time to pause and re-think.

Regulators have developed their requirements with good reason. There may be something in their prescription that isn't quite right for your organisation if implemented literally and with no thought, but their recommendations will be based on their experiences of what can go wrong, and what other companies have done to resolve those problems.

If what you are doing is just following a paint-by-numbers approach to meet a set of regulatory mandates, you are almost certainly missing the point. Every investment you make should be delivering some kind of return or positive business benefit. Effective data management can deliver transformational value, if done properly; or can be an astounding waste of money, and still not meet your regulator's expectations, if done badly.

What are you doing to make sure your investments in data management for regulatory compliance purposes are also driving positive business outcomes?

Working With People Who 'Get It'

Working with people who "get it" is a joy.

No need to spend lots of time explaining basic concepts, no need to persuade and "sell the benefits"... just straight to the point.

It makes everything easier.

The reality is though, even when you are lucky enough to be working with people who do "get it", there will always be plenty of people who don't.

This includes people who are very supportive of what you need to do, they just don't understand what it will take to do those things...

This is why, on any Data Management initiative, especially when it is ambitious and large scale (and will therefore require investment and prioritisation), the ability to engage effectively with people who don't really "get it" is crucial to success.

As a senior Data Leader, this will always be part of your role, so it's a skill that is worth practicing.

It's also worth acknowledging that it will always be the case. Rather than getting frustrated, it's better to learn to enjoy it and see it as a core part of your role.

Are you lucky enough to be working with people who "get it"?

What are you doing to engage with those who don't?

DATA VALUE SUCCESS v1.0

How To Get Back On Track

Do you feel like you've lost your way on your Data initiative?

Like you're working really hard but it's not having any real impact?

You're doing "the things" in the plan, and everyone's pouring their time and energy in, but it's somehow missing the point?

It's time to revisit your target business outcomes and success measures.

If you don't already have some agreed, take a step back and write them down.

How is the work you are doing going to deliver them?

Take a moment to review where you are going.

Communicate the end goals to your team and stakeholders.

Remind each other *WHY* you are doing what you are doing.

And if there's anything you are doing that isn't going to help you achieve your business outcomes, then stop working on those things and re-focus your efforts on things that will.

There is no such thing as a bad time to review how you are prioritising your efforts, to make sure your are driving in the right direction.

Even if you uncover that you have been on the wrong path for a while, better to find out now and course-correct than to continue to waste time and to store up re-work and unnecessary costs for the future.

What are you doing, to align everything you do, to the business outcomes that you are working towards?

Keep Going!

Consistency, Discipline and Persistence.

Sometimes that's all it takes to succeed in Data Management.

Should you look for opportunities to be more efficient and automate things? Yes, absolutely.

But some things just require a relentless commitment to high standards, regardless of the technological or organisational disadvantages that you are working to overcome.

Sometimes it can feel like a thankless and never-ending task; and sometimes you may feel like you've slid backwards and are struggling to re-build momentum; but in those times of struggle, remember the vision. Remember the value and benefit of what you are doing.

Keep going. It's worth the effort, if you stick with it. Persist and you will eventually succeed.

Conclusion

We Can Always Improve

Thank you for reading. I hope you enjoyed the book and got a huge amount of value out of it.

As you made your way through its pages, you may have noticed several themes running throughout, and this was no accident.

Often the simplest and most obvious truths about how to do things successfully are missed, as people over-complicate things or focus on things that seem important at face value, but are in fact nothing more than distractions from the things that really matter.

If there is one message that I hope you take away, it is to **always start by working out what outcome you are aiming for, and then make sure everything you do is aimed at delivering that outcome**.

Then, once you've started towards your target outcome, **keep going**.

If you find yourself off track: pause, correct your aim, and get going again.

No matter what the subject is, this basic principle holds true: **success is found through persistent work towards the right goal.**

However, no matter how clear your goal and how good your aim, there will be times when you find yourself off track. There will be times where you make mistakes, or find that something that worked before doesn't work anymore, or even find that the outcome you were aiming for is no longer the right one.

Each time this happens, it is an opportunity to learn and improve.

And this is the other key to Data Management success, just as it is for everything else in our lives: **continuous improvement**.

Not doing things once and thinking we're all done.

Also, knowing that things will inevitably change, and we will always need to adapt and try new things and leverage new technologies to stay on the front foot.

If you live by these principles, and are able to apply some of the tips that are provided throughout this book, you are definitely going to be on the right track.

So, here's to your well planned, continuously improving Data Management journey!

Acknowledgements

My first 'thanks' has got to go to the amazing network of professionals on LinkedIn, who I have had the opportunity to share ideas with and learn from over the past few years. It's been their engagement and encouragement, which kept me posting, and led me to have such a lot of good and proven content readily available to build into this book.

Next, I'd like to thank my colleagues in the Baringa Data, Analytics and Artificial Intelligence practice, who are an incredibly talented group of people, are brilliant fun to work with, and have been super supportive of me in this journey.

I'd also like to thank my clients: it's great to be able to make a real difference at work, and it's even better when the people the work is for, are all so intelligent and nice to work with.

And of course, I would also like to thank my friends, family and children, who are the most important people in the world to me and always deserve acknowledgement!

About The Author

Paul Jones is a senior executive and data expert, who's been working on and around data transformation initiatives, including building data teams and Chief Data Offices, since the early 2000's.

He advises Boards and CxO-level stakeholders on how to realise the strategic value of data and how to translate theory into practical outcomes.

Paul is passionate about mentoring and coaching people to succeed and gets great pleasure in sharing his knowledge and helping others.

http://www.pauldanieljones.com

http://www.linkedin.com/in/pauldanieljonesuk/

Please Provide A Review!

If you enjoyed this book, I would really appreciate it if you **please provide a review on Amazon.**

It will help raise awareness for other people who will get value from it.

Many thanks!

amazon.com
★★★★★

Please Follow Me!

Also, if you got value from the content here, please do follow me on LinkedIn, for more content on driving value through Data Management.

www.linkedin.com/in/**pauldanieljonesuk**/

If You Liked This Book...

You might also like my other book, "The Data Garden And Other Data Allegories".

It's a set of **6 fictional stories**, which bring to life key Data Management topics, in interesting ways.

The stories include:
- The Data Garden
- The Data Governance Country
- The Data Quality Hospital
- The Data Architecture Construction Project
- The Metadata Mess
- The Data Literacy Driving School

You can find it on Amazon, in Kindle and Paperback formats.

www.ingramcontent.com/pod-product-compliance
Lightning Source LLC
Chambersburg PA
CBHW071358210526
45465CB00001B/152